# Christian Höller

# *Time Action Vision*



JRP|RINGIER & LES PRESSES DU RÉEL

# Christian Höller

*Time Action Vision*

*Conversations in Cultural Studies, Theory, and Activism*

EDITED BY ANNE-JULIE RACCOURSIER
RESEARCH-BASED MASTER PROGRAMME
CCC—CRITICAL CURATORIAL CYBERMEDIA,
GENEVA UNIVERSITY OF ART AND DESIGN/
HAUTE ÉCOLE D'ART ET DE DESIGN – GENÈVE

# Table of Contents

## *Foreword*
## Anne-Julie Raccoursier

*Time Action Vision*, the title of which plays on a programmatic song by the punk group Alternative TV,[1] brings together twelve conversations held by Christian Höller between 1996 and 2006 with theoreticians and activists critically engaged in the cultural field. Not only do they trace a substantial part of Christian Höller's editorial practice and his range of interests over a period of ten years, but they have also been an important source of material for his teaching in the field of Cultural Studies and on issues related to globalization and popular culture in the CCC Postgraduate Study Program[2] at the Geneva University of Art and Design [Haute école d'art et de design – Genève].

Since its creation in 1999, the CCC Program has been committed to developing a learning community that gathers teachers and students around critical studies (*études critiques*). The program encourages the theoretical and critical study of practices, institutions and discourses that constitute the field of culture. It is engaged in a continuous dialogue with an international network of artists, curators and academics. As one of the program's numerous resources, Cultural Studies has become an extremely stimulating model, particularly for the definition of culture, fields of study and inventive methodologies as they have developed since their origin at the CCCS (Centre for Contemporary Cultural Studies) in Birmingham. The CCCS's approach of maintaining a strong relationship with the time and political context in which theory is being written, discussed and developed makes it a useful tool in addressing the relationship between theory and practice, and looking at art in relation to its contemporary surroundings.

As stated by Cary Nelson, Paula A. Treichler and Lawrence Grossberg, Cultural Studies, "unlike traditional humanism, rejects the exclusive equation of culture with high culture and argues that all forms of cultural production need to be studied in relation to other cultural practices and to social and historical structures. Cultural Studies is thus committed to the study of the entire range of a society's arts, beliefs, institutions, and communicative practices."[3] In this perspective, then, culture encompasses ideas, attitudes, languages, practices, institutions and structures of power, as well as artistic forms, texts, architecture, mass-produced commodities and so forth.

A fundamental characteristic at the core of Cultural Studies is its interdisciplinary mode, which is present both in its objects of study and in the wide range of methodologies and cognitive or investigational tools adopted: "Its methodology, ambiguous from the beginning, could best be seen as bricolage ..."[4] But the main contributors to the field have also always stressed that Cultural Studies is not just anything: it is defined around a commitment and an engagement. And although Cultural Studies is open to an ever-widening scope of study, and constantly developing and being re-evaluated, it "shares a commitment to examining cultural practices from the point of view of their intrication with, and within, relations of power."[5]

The extension of the definition of culture, questions of critical engagement, and issues of power and identity, as well as historical and political contextualization, are a fantastic resource for a place of education trying to create awareness and a critical positioning. Stuart Hall's description of the Birmingham project is a vivid model: "At Birmingham, a central goal was to enable people to understand what was going on, and especially to provide ways of thinking, strategies of survival and resources of resistance."[6]

The expansion of the subjects of study and the development of Cultural Studies in the Anglo-Saxon academic world have been phenomenal, whereas it took a long time before interest in the field grew in the French-speaking realm. Among the many reasons for the persistent resistance to Cultural Studies to be found in the French context, even though—paradoxically—French intellectuals have largely contributed to its development, one could cite the scientific approach toward the validation of theory, as well as the strong republican and universalist models which are not ready to be questioned and challenged by multiple voices and heterogeneous methodologies. Cultural Studies has had the merit of politicizing theory by directly questioning the institutions of knowledge and the scientific measurement associated with disciplines, and by opening a discussion about the politics at large embodied in culture.

Taking as its starting point some of the authors and main characteristics of Cultural Studies, this publication is "a collection of conversations" that expands way beyond what is usually defined as Cultural Studies and explores many realms around contemporary cultural practices and theory. At no point when the interviews were conducted was there the intention to publish them together. They have been part of Christian Höller's contributions to the Austrian and German art magazines *springerin* and *Texte zur Kunst*, as well as following his ongoing interest in issues of globalization, popular culture and activism. The result is a rather heterogeneous range of positions, references, works and discussions recorded over a period of ten years, which in this publication enter into a dialogue with one another.

The first part, a set of three conversations, introduces the specific field of Cultural Studies. Stuart Hall provides some insights into its beginning and genealogy at the CCCS in Birmingham and delineates some important points of departure for his own explorations of identity and postcolonialism. Both through his theoretical work and his political and pedagogical commitment, he is an exemplary figure of an intellectual accentuating the emancipative aspect of knowledge, especially when we consider his later association with the Open University[7] and the many useful pedagogical publications in which he was deeply involved.

Lawrence Grossberg, an American who studied in Birmingham, has made a large contribution to the development of Cultural Studies overseas. In the conversation included here, he describes the manifold relations between culture and neoconservatism in the United States and how some cultural tendencies of the 1960s and 1970s have been used and articulated as political strategies. Grossberg explains, for instance, how some crucial features of popular music with respect to energy and emotion have been re-used in communication mechanisms and disciplinary processes.

Meaghan Morris, starting out from an Australian and Oceanic point of view, reflects upon the development of Cultural Studies as an apparently widening theoretical stream. She analyzes misconceptions of Cultural Studies as an approach toward "global culture" and elaborates on its relations with issues of institutionalization, historicity and contextualization. As she says, "There is no such thing as 'global culture,' except in the professional imaginary of cultural theorists who write about other theorists without doing empirical research; there are only concrete contexts in which global products are taken up in particular ways."

In the second section, Paul Gilroy, Achille Mbembe and Ella Shohat, from very different perspectives, give us an insight into their engagement with postcolonialism. Paul Gilroy's argument is that, within the new parameters of globalization (new modes of life, greater mobility, migration, hybridity) that have changed our world, we are still stuck in old views and assumptions about race and racism. He urges us to revise the paradigms of raciology in order to fight against the recurrence of racism and nationalist formations, but also to prevent a re-enactment of ethnic fears that do not take into account the changes that occurred in the second half of the 20th century.

Achille Mbembe focuses on developments in Africa and observes the working of culture on this huge continent still struggling both with the aftermath of colonization and the move toward globalization. In his book *On the Postcolony*, he speaks about how power in most African countries has been and is still operated through a formation of will, fantasy and passions that, through repetition, become an authoritative narrative. His attempt is to navigate between these powerful narratives and the feeling of victimization in a bid to find possibilities to re-appropriate power and make it operative through culture.

Ella Shohat, with her biographical experience of displacement, has developed her theoretical work at the intersection of several fields of research such as gender, postcolonial and media studies in order to challenge the Western hegemony in the cultural sphere. Her critique of Eurocentrism is targeted at the ways in which historical systems of knowledge have ideologically been based on and thus have fostered European supremacy. By explaining her approach toward "multiculturalism" as well as her critique of "Eurocentric feminism," she urges critical artists and thinkers "to re-engage the hegemonic narrative by which aesthetics and history are taught and create new ways of knowing."

The third section presents two visions of globalization. To distinguish between globalization as a condition, a process and a political project and to avoid perceiving it as a magical course, David Harvey, who roots his theoretical work in the analysis of geography, introduces the conceptual device of "historical-geographical materialism." Geography is both a real material component in the development of capitalism and a site that encrypts its actions and workings. Harvey underlines certain contradictions or tensions inherent in capitalism that are maybe best visible in the geographical landscape: on the one hand, the search for ever greater fluidity and mobility of capital and on the other, the materiality of the geography which fixes class inequalities in the landscape and makes visible the materiality of transportation and communication devices enabling the flux of "immaterial" capital.

The renowned sociologist Zygmunt Bauman, in his characteristic way, focuses on issues of mobility and global migration. In the context of global structures of power, the possibilities of agency for human beings are strongly restricted and "freedom to mobility," both geographically and socially, becomes the mark of people's status in the social world. To analyze the inequalities with respect to mobility, he introduces two figures, the tourist and the vagabond/refugee, as two new classes in the global era. These two figures especially help in thinking about the issue of frontiers, both real and symbolic, which, beyond questions of national identity and nationhood, strongly govern the conduct of human beings.

The last section brings together four positions questioning the possibilities of "participation" in our contemporary world. By presenting very diverse experiences, works and accounts, and comparing the shifts that have occurred between different decades, these four conversations explore issues connected with being an actor of transformation. Moreover, all the interviewees attempt to negotiate the borders between culture, activism and citizenship, and critically engage with the notion of audience and its potential.

Tariq Ali has published widely on the development in the Middle East as well as the current political situation there. As a long-time editor of *New Left Review*, he represents a sort of political "continuity" from the 1960s until today. In the short interview included here, he gives a striking testimony to the current state of crisis and the violence and recolonization enacted toward the Middle East, as well as many of their symbolic occurrences as conveyed by Western media.

Bill Ayers was a central figure in activist movement "Weather Underground," which in the 1960s and 1970s committed many acts of symbolic violence against American governmental institutions in protest at the war in Vietnam. Under the slogan "Bringing the war back home," this group's actions opened up a lot of questions about dissent and resistance by the citizens of a country to the action taken by its government abroad. Today, Bill Ayers is a professor of education who has written on the importance of creating progressive educational opportunities in urban public schools. His interview, which was conducted shortly after September 11 and followed the publication of his memoir *Fugitive Days*, brings into perspective two very different time periods that nevertheless seem to share some common constituents.

The filmmaker and theoretician Jean-Pierre Gorin traces the activities of the "Group Dziga Vertov," which he founded together with Jean-Luc Godard in 1968 and which operated through the early 1970s. He relates their attempts at that time to define and produce a distinctly *political* cinema and also talks about their experiments with (other) distribution possibilities and audiences. In addition, Gorin projects a trajectory of film with a political edge from the 1960s until the present day.

Finally, Irit Rogoff, who is professor of Visual Culture at Goldsmiths College, addresses issues of visuality and participation. Rogoff has for many years been collaborating with artists and activists to expand the field of art in interdisciplinary ways, both in theory and practice. The conversation revolves around her idea of visual culture, and issues of performativity and subjectivity. It also addresses her investigation of new modes of knowledge and strategies of empowerment, which figure centrally in her current research project on audience participation in contemporary art spaces.

In some of his writings not included here,[8] Christian Höller describes three aspects of his encounter with Cultural Studies as having been the discovery of a methodology usable in a variety of contexts; an active engagement that enables a dialogue with what is happening in our world culturally and politically; and finally, an affinity with culture which is both thought- and action-provoking and empowers us to be part of our world and culture as participants.

We hope that this publication will encourage and stimulate its readers to venture more deeply into the works of the individual authors. We also hope that the various topics and positions touched upon within the wide scope of this book will provide them with perspectives for investigating their own heterogeneous life-world and time, not least as critical participants.

We are very grateful to all the authors and interview partners, especially for their generosity in sharing their knowledge and perspectives during sometimes quite labor-intensive processes. Most of the conversations included here (Grossberg, Morris, Gilroy, Mbembe, Harvey, Bauman, Ayers, Ali, Gorin) are reprinted with the kind permission of *springerin* magazine, which commissioned them in the first place but was only able to publish them, sometimes in edited form, in German. A shortened German version of the conversation with Stuart Hall appeared in the journal *Texte zur Kunst* in 1996. The interviews with Ella Shohat and Irit Rogoff appear for the first time in this book.

Finally, we would like to kindly acknowledge the Geneva University of Art and Design [Haute école d'art et de design – Genève] for its support in the realization of this publication.

[1] The actual title of Alternative TV is "Action Time Vision," on *The Image Has Cracked – The First Album by Alternative TV*, Deptford Fun City Records, 1978.
[2] Since Fall 2008, the name of the Program is Research-Based Master Programme CCC—Critical Curatorial Cybermedia.
[3] "Cultural Studies: An Introduction, " in Cary Nelson, Paula A. Treichler, Lawrence Grossberg (eds.), *Cultural Studies*. New York/London: Routledge 1992, p. 4.
[4] Ibid., p. 2.
[5] Ibid., p. 3 (quotation of Tony Bennett).
[6] Stuart Hall, "The Emergence of Cultural Studies and the Crisis of the Humanities," in *October* 53 (1990), p. 22.
[7] The Open University is an open academic educational institution spread decentrally all over Great Britain for students who are mostly in the workforce.
[8] Cf. Christian Höller, "Offene Blockaden – geschlossene Transfers. Anmerkungen zur aktuellen Cultural Studies-Rezeption," in *springerin – Hefte für Gegenwartskunst*, 1/1998, p. 30-34 and "Konsolidierungsschwächen. Zum anhaltenden Cultural Studies-Boom," in *Texte zur Kunst*, No. 35 (September 1999), p. 139-142.

CHAPTER I

# On Cultural Studies

# *Terrains of Disturbance*
# Conversation with Stuart Hall

Interview conducted in September 1996.

Stuart Hall is considered, and probably justifiably so, as the person who has most continuously helped to shape and correct the Cultural Studies discourse over the past three-and-a-half decades. Since his emigration from Jamaica to Great Britain in 1951, he has often been found in central and crucial positions in this field: in the late 1950s as editor of the magazine *New Left Review*, and then from 1964 at the Birmingham Centre for Contemporary Cultural Studies (CCCS). From 1968 to 1979, he was then himself director of the Centre. It was during this period that a large part of the British subculture studies appeared, later to be called the first phase of Cultural Studies. In 1979—the controversies (e.g. feminist and ethnic controversies) within the Centre had meanwhile multiplied—he left Birmingham and went on to the Open University, a kind of open academic educational institution spread de-centrally all over Great Britain for students who are mostly in the workforce. After retiring in 1998, Stuart Hall is still affiliated with this institution besides being a guest professor at London's Goldsmith's College and being part of the directorial board of the Institute of International Visual Arts (InIVA).

CH *One of the main realms of Cultural Studies, as well as one of the main areas that you have been concerned with over a long period of time, was the discourse or politics of identity. As a way of approaching that topic, I wanted to ask you if you could sum up, retrospectively, when and how this issue of identity first came up, and what developments of discourse necessitated it. How useful was it at a certain time, and what shortcomings have there been?*

SH I think the genealogy of the question of identity in Cultural Studies is a rather complex one and I don't know that anybody has really correctly mapped it. "Identity talk," let me put it that way, is now very present, including in very traditional curricula such as political science and many other disciplines. It is hard to remember where it came from. But just to put it very simply, in the early stages of Cultural Studies we were interested in culture as shared meanings, notions of shared meanings, and it did therefore have a kind of collective feel, it was about communities, groups, subcultures, etc. It wasn't really a matter of subjective identity or identifications. On the other hand, to emphasize the cultural as opposed to just the social is to turn attention to questions of meaning and questions of how individuals make sense of themselves and their world. It opens up the issue that this isn't given, written in the stars, inscribed in our class identities or national belongings. It is something that is an active set of practices to produce cultural meaning. So I suppose that the attention to culture opened a space in which, later on, issues about identity were discussed. But if you look at the very early work of Cultural Studies, I don't think you will see identity named in that way as an essential topical concern.

Another element is the critique of essentialist and determinist modes of thought, which has always played a crucial role in Cultural Studies right from the very beginning. Even when Cultural Studies was at its most Marxist, it always stopped short of fully deterministic ways of understanding culture—by that I mean that if you could just understand the socio-economic location of a particular group, you could read off from that what their values or meaning were, their dominant ideology. Cultural Studies were always suspicious of the lack of complexity in the understanding of the symbolic and interpretative world of groups. The moment you step away from a prescriptive or deterministic model, you have to ask what the processes are by which individuals find themselves attached to or called upon by ideologies or discourses. So the issue of identification is there even before you have fully named it, for example in its psychoanalytic meaning. It is a quite complex process that is not automatic: why for instance do some working-class people feel positively about the market? Why do other working-class people identify differently?

Another way of putting the genealogy is to think its relation to Marxism: If Cultural Studies had ever been a brand of classical Marxism, I don't think the issue of identification or identity would ever have arisen. Identity is not prescribed in classical Marxism! You more or less know what your identity is supposed to be, and if you don't know you are suffering from false consciousness. Identity is not an issue here. It is more of a problem to get you to have the consciousness you ought to have, but that's not a complicated problem of analysis. Cultural Studies always had a very troublesome, complex and difficult relationship with such essentialist and reductionist models. Especially with Marxism, the boundary is quite troublesome, because Marxism was asking questions about power that Cultural Studies were interested in, but it was asking them in a way which didn't take culture seriously in all its symbolic dimensions.

If you put that in the political context, a lot of questions arise about the politics of the 1970s and 1980s, when all the prescriptive identifications suddenly collapsed—in 1979 and 1983, more working-class people who were unemployed voted for Mrs. Thatcher than for the Labour Party. Something must be wrong with our understanding of what subjective identification is all about and how cultural and social identities are being occupied if you don't understand something quite as fundamental as that, which was, after all, the watershed for all political parties in the 1980s.

Also, you have to take into consideration questions of feminism, which from the very beginning affirmed that "the personal is political." This meant that questions of personal choice, personal identity and personal subjectivity were issues that could be discussed within a political and theoretical framework. All in all, there is a kind of long march to the questions of identity emerging with the kind of centrality that they have acquired in recent years.

*In an influential essay,[1] you wrote that the feminist intervention on the one hand and issues of ethnicity and racism on the other were the two main disruptions taking place in the history of Cultural Studies. I actually wanted to touch upon this question later but maybe we can pick it up right now: wasn't it with these two interventions, feminist and ethnic, that the need for wider political articulations was somehow lost or temporarily shifted out of sight because these issues occupied huge spaces, center-stage, so to speak? Or to put another way: do you think retrospectively, historically and theoretically that these two big interventions could be accommodated within a largely Gramscian perspective of Cultural Studies, which was always one of its leading tendencies?*

The interventions of feminism and the interventions around race and ethnicity were major interventions in the life of the Centre for Cultural Studies.[2] They've been much talked about and I have identified them because they have long-running historical consequences. Their impact on the field has been to change it decisively. They are also important because they connected Cultural Studies with much wider social movements that were going on outside academia. But they weren't by any means the only interventions. One of the reasons why I identified them is because they represented a break with a long period in which they were assumed to be just questions of class. Whether in a Marxist framework or not, sociologically, class was the articulation with culture and power that we were principally interested in. Therefore, questions of capitalism and culture, those old Frankfurt School questions about mass culture, the Americanization of Western societies and the world, capitalism and consequently the distribution of cultures by class were sort of taken for granted.

Feminism and race were not the only interventions. So, for example, many people would say that the most important intervention was structuralism and semiotics, which caused a break with the Williams/Hoggart kind of English humanism. Equally important was the struggle with Althusser … and Gramsci. Two things about Gramsci: he was never the universally accepted model in the Centre. In that period, for instance, most feminists were not Gramscians. They regarded Gramsci as someone holding on to last residues that had long become questionable. The overall picture was always much more pluralist than that. You could say that in that very same period, psychoanalysis made an appearance and is another field that has had a major impact. It's just a matter of: you tell the story and you make it seem more seamless, more universal, more integrated than it actually was. This has partly to do with the organization of the Centre: there were six or seven working groups and they sort of had an identity on their own. I was involved in the subculture and the media one. Each one had a sort of sub-area of intellectual concerns within it. That was the kind of framework in which Cultural Studies was the critical discipline. It asked questions about power and later on, questions about subjectivity. But it wasn't an attempt to create a kind of Gramscian orthodoxy. I would say Gramsci was important in the sense that those people who were interested in the interface between Cultural Studies and Marxism found in Gramsci the most acceptable version they could work with for a while. Gramsci for us was the limit case about Althusserism. We could go to Althusser up to the point where he broke altogether from notions of practice and social world because he wanted to erect Big Theory as a kind of autonomous realm, and that's the point where most of us stopped believing *Lire "Le Capital."* We came to the view that Gramsci was as far as we could go, still to ask the questions of capitalism, culture and class without falling into a reductionist mode. People who wanted to work in that mode found "Gramscianism" a position to hold, but it wasn't a sort of orthodoxy. This is not in any sense to refuse your question. As you can imagine, in an intellectual outfit like this what you choose to talk about and read and the paradigms you choose to work in have enormous consequences. You get to see certain alignments and you don't see others.

You might very well ask, for example, "Where is the whole question about ecology and nature?" Well, it never surfaced very strongly. It's not that nobody was interested in it, but it never became a pertinent object of intellectual practice and concern. Other people elsewhere came by different routes, for instance, from Hegel and the debate about nature; they got into ecology immediately and never left it. Another point worth making is that although Cultural Studies were first named in the Centre, we never imagined that it was Cultural Studies that we were doing. We were aware that they had arisen out of very fortuitous circumstances and brought together a rather arbitrary collection of disciplines. I was trained in literature, deserting literature for a kind of cultural anthropology. Richard Hoggart came from literature, Richard Johnson came from history, and we all read some sociology. But there is no reason why Cultural Studies should have started out of literature, art history or formal semiotics. We were aware that we could ask the same kinds of questions in different settings and this might have produced different sets of articulations. In those days, we were rather modest about our ambitions. It's only subsequently that Cultural Studies have plotted to take over the world … [laughs]. Of course, the articulations were specific and followed a very particular dynamic and patterned pathway.

## Identity One and Identity Two

*Coming back once again to the politics of identity, I would like to follow up on my first question: up to which point did it really prove useful to stage questions in terms of identity and difference, and when did the point arise when people said: "Maybe it's getting too separatist, leaving out a kind of broader picture"? Didn't the whole development of the discourse lead to an increasing separatist fragmentation, with people being concerned only with questions of representation, how they wanted to represent themselves, and how they didn't want to be represented?*

There are two different strands put together in the question you're asking. First of all, let me respond to the question about usefulness and the negative aspects of identity discourse. I would say that it was extremely useful in opening up all kinds of questions which had been effectively closed down or rendered invisible by the assumption that those connections could only be made from within a certain class basis. Now, the historical context of all this was the 1960s. This was a period in which, outside of the Centre, the traditional agencies of social change were entering a kind of stasis. More and more, politics was being carried by the so-called new social movements: by feminism, by the peace movement, by the beginning of race politics, by the opening of the Civil Rights struggle in the US. What was moving politically were these community groups, and in contrast to the political parties, which were huge bureaucratic organizations, these were movements of choice and consent. Nobody obliged you to join in. You didn't have to be a member of CND[3] to vote, you were a member of CND because you identified with it and the more you identified with it, the more you discovered that all kinds of people with different identities were there, too: young people, people in transition from one class to another, scholarship boys with a working-class background. All sorts of transitional people were driven to these movements and not only political movements, also movements in culture. In the 1960s, it was the Beatles and the big explosion of British rock music that brought together people with different backgrounds. A lot of them were kids from art schools with working-class backgrounds, kids who went to college and dropped out, and who were more like street intellectuals. So the whole political game that we were trying to study was getting enormously complicated. What was moving right up and through the Vietnam War and 1968 in France were these movements that didn't have any clear given class identity, any clear position in the political spectrum. The question of identity, "Where do you belong?" was answered in ways like, "I am doing this because I'm a peacenik, because I'm a woman, because I'm black etc." I think in that period Cultural Studies would have been locked in the past if it hadn't in some way tried to study those movements and in a way identify with them, politically. What happens then is that you're getting into a second phase where you begin to see the limits of this approach …

*Didn't you at one point identify an "identity politics one" and an "identity politics two"?*[4]

Yes. I'm talking exactly about that transition and what I just described was "identity politics one." "Identity politics two" is the awareness that every identity is also an exclusion, and that within every identity there are also differences. First of all, there isn't a wider politics to be had from that kind of political movement, because how do men identify with women's struggles? How do whites identify with black struggle? How do you put together any sorts of politics which isn't simply moving around from one issue to another? For a time, it seemed to us that the people were belonging to a "stage army of the good." On Saturday, you put on your peacenik uniform and on Sunday you went to the anti-racist meeting … moving around from one identity to another. So you start to wonder, "Who are all these people? What are all these things? Which of them are they in which moment of the week, on what day?"

This leads to the idea that identity is much more complex, that it is internally differentiated, that it's contradictory and that it doesn't settle down, that people are one thing one day and change their mind tomorrow. Organizational weaknesses begin to be identified at this point. There is a very important moment in feminism called the "tyranny of structurelessness." A famous pamphlet written by Sheila Rowbotham and others called *Beyond the Fragments*[5] raises the question that if everybody only goes to their designated identity groups, what sort of politics is that? The result might be to push into different directions. One is to say, "This is a dead end. Don't ask this question anymore. Let us go back to the state, the distribution of wealth, material issues etc."

Another option is to recognize that the questions being posed around identity and identification are of crucial importance, but that they can't be the only questions. They alone will not resolve the problem, because there are fixed identities so that, politically and theoretically, black women might say to white feminists, "Am I a feminist? I'm black. In the black context, you and I have different interests. In the feminist cause, though, you and I might share an interest against my own black man." This means that identities are at least situational, depending on which issue is in the forefront, which demonstration is going on, if race is on the top of the agenda, etc. With this, you get a much more complex political scene. It's not that identification is not an issue, because in my view, without identification no folks show up in any places. There is no reason why anybody should come out at all unless there is something that makes an investment worthwhile. So there has to be identification and I'm more and more interested in the process of identification, which is complicated and which is not fixed once and for all, never stitched up, never tied. I'm more interested in that than I am in identities as a kind of finished end product of this process. Once you think you're there, the next thing that happens is that you change, you give it up.

So I haven't taken the line that this is a dead end altogether and that one should give it up. Instead, I've tried to recast those questions by looking at other dimensions as well. However, even that second position is open to the critique that you're making, which is that it is still preoccupied with questions of subjectivity, identity from inside the subject, cultural meaning, representation, etc. What about the big bad world? Global capitalism? And I actually think that this is a genuine question, a big problem that Cultural Studies have to face. How can one recover some of these questions without thinking them in the old reductionist ways, and without losing hold of the very profound insights we've gained into the importance of subjective representational meanings? In that sense, I don't give up what I would call "the cultural terrain," by which I mean that all the human practices we are interested in take place within meaning. It does not mean that there is nothing but meaning, but rather that there is no human practice that doesn't have a dimension of meaning to it.

*Maybe one more remark about this obsession with identity and differentiation which came up now: this may be a very crude comparison, but in a way, something like this has also happened with the reformulation and re-conceptualization of national identities and the rising nationalism accompanying it. I don't know whether there is a more profound parallel to that, but in most European countries when there is talk of cultural identity, it is automatically assumed that it is a particular* national *identity that is at stake. I was wondering whether the discourse of identity hasn't long been taken up by neoconservatives …*

I don't' know whether it was that particular discourse that was taken up in that way. I think people who have been interested in the centrality of national or ethnic facts, in the constitution of social groups and their practices, have always thought about cultural identity in one way or another as an important element. But I think that the connection you're making does hold in a certain respect: if you stick with "identity politics one," the first definition of identity as we discussed it in the old days, there is no stopping point between saying, "Well, all women should stick together," "All whites stick together," "All Germans stick together," and so on. I think it's exactly the move to the second form of identity ("identity politics two") where you see that there is always a question of identity at stake, but not a question of finished, completed, single and un-contradictory identities. When you get to that point you have a way of opening up the recuperation of the identity question, back to a kind of conservative position. Underneath that is a methodological principle which I think is very important, viz. that there isn't any guarantee against that kind of recuperation.[6] I've seen it too long, radical practices falling off, being recaptured and reconstituted before you notice it, being rearticulated into something else. But that can't prevent us from holding on to dangerous territories. You do watch how something is being appropriated, but to say, "I use it this way," is invaluable in such a situation. I have used that methodological principle again and again because it is exactly the same way as Derrida says, "We are at the end of Western metaphysics, but unfortunately, there is nothing to think with except those very Western metaphysical concepts." This is the rational course of thinking in postmodern times as inevitably a sort of deconstructive time, as more and more concepts become usable outside the organic, positive paradigms in which they have been originally constructed. There has to be deconstructive critique and then you have to go back and recuperate some of the fragments, which you try to use in a sort of non-theological way. Identity is certainly one of those. I would think about identity questions now as a terrain of disturbance that you have to go on asking about, rather than a concept that is settled and that you can happily apply.

## Hybridity

*Maybe we can move on to a second area now, the area of hybridity, or "impure cultural identities," as this notion might also be circumscribed. As I understood you, your anti-essentialist impulses led you to reformulate questions of identity in terms of hybrid forms. As a kind of entry point to this area I was wondering how that kind of cultural hybridity is different from the postmodernist flirting with nomads and nomadism? And secondly, could you briefly elaborate on the specific empirical and historical conditions that gave rise to the notion of hybridity?*

For me, these two questions are very closely connected. Hybridity is another way of rethinking cultural identity in a non-essentialist way. What I am interested in is first of all cultures which manifestly work, in the sense of providing meaning—through which people make sense of their lives—and which are obviously not the product of a single, organic formation. I'm interested in that because I belong to one myself; the Caribbean is archetypically a hybrid culture. It has no origin because the people who lived there were wiped out by the Spanish over 150 years ago, so there is no indigenous culture. The same is not true if you go to Latin America. In the main lands, there are many indigenous peoples, but I only know very few indigenous people in the majority of the Caribbean islands. Everybody there came from somewhere else, from Portugal, from France, from Spain, from Holland, from England, from Africa, from India and so on. That is why it is a hybrid culture. I got into the "culture question" myself by trying to understand how such a culture works, sort of assuming that cultures were organic things; this was clearly not one. People in the early 1950s and 1960s who came from that area thought that they had a permanent identity problem, that they would never know who they were because the only people who know who they are are people who come from an organic or historically lived culture. So I started to think whether this was the case or not. That's the empirical background that lies behind it.

Then there was a second move in which we tried to convince ourselves that we came from a culture like any other, that we had all sorts of problems in it, and we started to ask what it could do for us. You might be surprised that I'm talking about culture in such an instrumental way, but in the 1960s and 1970s, second-generation black kids in Britain who no longer could go back to the Caribbean and who suffered tremendous racism and discrimination here were actually *saved* by culture. They found a way through Bob Marley and Rastafarianism not to commit social suicide, which is what slaves did. They jumped out of ships because they couldn't see themselves living any longer. Young people in the 1960s and 1970s were on the edge of a kind of collective social suicide and they were saved by finding a way in which they could live with themselves, rediscovering their history, finding that they did have a connection with Africa, a very old place, and so on. This was the way in which I saw culture working.

We have a hybrid culture. Most cultures are unified, but then you have to ask, "Since when? Unified in what way? Which of the European cultures is homogeneous in that way?" What you find out is that it's usually a patchwork of bits and pieces stitched together. If you consider "Englishness," you will find that it is not an expression of a unified organic culture, but rather an attempt to stitch up and hold together what you would have to describe as differentiated cultures, contradictory, all over the place. One after the other, you can unpack these different ingredients in history. When did Spain as a unified culture emerge? Is it Moorish Spain, Catholic Spain, the Franco regime, what else? What is this unified Hispanic culture that has constituted culture identities by which people could live? This is a move to open up the existing world, but then you have to ask the question —just like you do with identity—"If they aren't unified, does this mean that they are nothing?" That's where the postmodernism question comes in, because postmodernism suggests that these are all meta-narratives, stories we tell ourselves about culture, that unity and identity is something that we spin just for the purpose of holding things together. They do not have any other substance. We are sort of lost in fragments and we can play, we can be whoever we are, whatever we choose. I do not think that is the case either, I think that there *is* some substance to identity and identification, but it isn't the unified thing that we talked about before. It isn't something that we could get a hold of. We rather have to ask how culture is *working*—provided that you don't think of it as something given in the genes or constructed by kinship or living in a homeland or sharing the same values from the beginning of time to the future.

So you have to think about culture in another way. The question of hybridity actually comes in as a sort of metaphorical tool, if you ask *not* how a few funny cultures happened to survive, but what culture *is* and how it generally works. Still, you have to place that question in a historical setting. In the setting of the 20th century you realize that there is more movement and migration between cultures, economic migration, civil wars, poverty, hunger, natural disasters, people on the move between cultures. Even if in the past there was a kind of sentiment that culture was a more settled formation, it certainly isn't so any longer. The culture we inhabit, partly technologically, because of satellites and modern communication systems, is breaking the link between identity and space, which is a very ancient one. The nation-state is the last moment when identity and place could be harnessed together. After that comes the satellite revolution and suddenly, people's identities are in the airwaves. They are not located by space anymore. Once you see that you are in a context in which these questions come up, this also provides you with a political cutting edge against what I think is the political reaction to the notion of hybridity, which is to try, in the face of all the evidence that I've been talking about, to nevertheless rescue an authentic German folk, an authentic German spirit, an authentic British spirit, against which you could symbolically mark who is in and who is out. That is why racism is not just something that we don't like, but it is absolutely endemic to a world in which migration and hybridity are spreading rapidly. In that situation, people are desperately fearful of losing their identities. They will get in the business of joining the line and saying, "Who belongs to us and who doesn't?"

*Coming back to the point about postmodernism, or the affinity between hybridity and postmodernist notions of fragmentation, you once claimed that the postcolonial condition prepared one perfectly for the postmodernist feel. Nevertheless, I am still interested in the differences between the two. Hybridity is obviously more than just postmodernist play, or a "voluntarist" concocting of elements.*

I think it is different in at least two senses. One has to do with something you just touched upon. Hybridity is not as "voluntarist" as I think the postmodernist ideal has it. Identities are not just open to choice. There are limits on them, there are determining factors, structures, etc. Secondly, not only are they like that, they *have to be* like that, because cultures are about meanings and meanings are always specific. The fact that you don't come from *one* set of meanings does not mean that you don't come from several sets of meanings or different parts of sets of meanings; and each of those are specific, they have their histories. If one of the sets of meanings you come out of is the experience of plantation slavery, it is not same as being a Hispanic ranger in the same Latin world. It's very different. So you are always drawn not to one but various specificities, which set a sort of determining limit. You have to think about culture as a sort of configuration of limits. It's not that it has a fixed boundary, but there are configurations of limits, which are also the configurations of articulation without which we couldn't speak. Because they are the parts of language we inhabit, they allow us to make certain kinds of music, certain kinds of crossovers, to paint certain kinds of pictures that draw on three or four cognitive worlds and so on. So there is a positive and a negative side to it. The one thing it is not is an open space or a supermarket shelf from which you could freely choose. Of course, consumerism and technological development do give us the illusion that we can "think Indian" today and "think average" tomorrow. But this is not productive in any way, at least not in a way that would sustain an identity over a period of time, to which you could attach some social project.

It's very similar to questions of relativism. You might think from what I've said that I'm a kind of cultural relativist—and of course, as opposed to the notion of mono-culture, I am a relativist—but the notion that cultures are equally distributed, that there are no power relations, that there is no dramatic power geometry between one culture and another is not to live in the world that we live in. So one has to think about configurations, dispositions, boundaries, and thresholds while not falling back on a limitary notion of culture.

*A theoretical question about the concept of hybridity concerns the fact that once you start to talk about hybrids or impure forms, you have to presuppose a moment in which there were pre-existing units or pre-existing essences which only later on came together, were mixed, etc. Isn't something like this going on theoretically, once you start talking about impurity?*

I know this argument and I think it is probably logically correct. What I would say about it is that I don't think there was ever a time when cultures were unified and homogeneous. But there is no question that in the medieval world, local cultures were much more settled. They were never impervious to external influences, but the external influences were much more modulated, they took a long time to have an impact. Just think about the length of time it took to get a message from one small medieval community to another. If you think about the relationship of Europe to the rest of the world, you do have to say that the compass voyages represent a new qualitative moment, that they open a contact between worlds which, as far as we know, had no major openings between one another for centuries before that. This does not need to presuppose that there was a moment before when everything was self-contained and homogeneous. What we talk about is a relatively rapid movement where hybridity, from being the characteristic of marginal contact zones throughout the world, becomes much more like what most cultures are at their centers. I think one can register that historical shift without talking about an end or an origin. But I admit that we are slightly caught in an ideological trap here and I don't quite see a way out of it. I suppose hybridity is mostly being used metaphorically, it's a kind of impure concept itself, and it's being used polemically. I use it in the way in which Salman Rushdie talks about mongrels, describing himself as belonging to a mongrel culture. This is the taking on of the negative as a kind of political statement, the taking on of impurity. Therefore, it's not necessarily an analytic concept you want to rest with forever. You're more interested in the kind of discursive work it does by interrupting the notion of essentialism. It's a kind of intervention in philosophy, rather than an analytic, positive concept.

*You said at some point in the 1980s, confronted with things going on in postmodernism, and I quote, "now that you all feel so dispersed … I find myself centered at last,"[7] adding, "welcome to migranthood." Was this only an autobiographical remark or is there a more general story to it, concerning a kind of re-centering that has taken place?*

It came out of an autobiographical occasion, when Salman Rushdie, Homi Bhabha and I discussed our experiences of migranthood at the Institute of Contemporary Art in London. We are all migrants, we all came to London a long time ago, from places that had very long historical connections with British society. The remark was also a response to the particular situation where there was a very English audience who were obviously motivated to deny their Englishness like crazy, in favor of showing us that they were impure. We had been wheeled in as the marginal folks describing what marginality was to these center folks, and now, everybody wanted to get this migrant, marginal feel. In a way, they were right, because from another point of view, if you think about it, marginality has been fantastically productive. The very point of marginality has produced work of extraordinary richness. If you wanted to be an artist, for instance, would you locate yourself in Englishness without any question and hope to make it to the Tate? It's a kind a claim for the 21st century, and it is the historical reality. People are buying into it, sometimes for good reasons, and sometime rather fashionably, but nevertheless, it is interesting that that should be a fashion in itself, because it almost seems like a contradiction in terms. Those are identities that people *don't* want to be. There was a moment when I registered that they could see where we were, not by definition in a place outside or on the edge, but a place from which a lot could be said because the world had turned in that way.

I also used the notion to talk about the paradoxical situation of young black kids in Britain. Many of them are marginal in economic terms, marginal in terms of professional training, in terms of opportunities of getting up the ladder, and yet they are envied because they seem to know some secret about pleasure, about music and the body, about the theater of the street that the rest of the world has lost. This isn't something new, it has been going on the whole 20th century. The whole rediscovery of primitivism is a kind of reworking of a notion that the West has sacrificed. Inside of that is a very odd myth—it's the myth that precisely identifies people from the periphery with nature, emotions, the body, that they don't have any minds or thoughts. This is a very dangerous terrain, but nevertheless it is very odd to see the people who are very eager to keep black kids in their marginal place still thinking they have some secret that they would like to get hold of. So I was trying to talk about this paradox. I was interested in the fact that young black kids have become culturally centered in the London of the 1980s and 1990s, while at the same time being largely unemployed. A very paradoxical setting ...

## Postcolonialism

*Let me move on to a more global territory and talk about postcolonialism for a moment, or the postcolonial condition, which you also spent a huge amount of energy writing about. My first question is whether there is really a distinctive realm of postcoloniality which applies to a large group of people and not just a circle of elite intellectuals living in London or New York. From a bigger perspective it still seems —and this is of course a polemical point—that most people nowadays still live under the very old forms of colonialism, or under new forms of colonialism which have emerged under the new global economic conditions. How do you see that?*

It would be irresponsible to deny that there is a kind of chic postcolonialism, which does indeed come from and is very much associated with a relatively small number of what one might describe in rather old language as "third-world intellectuals." These intellectuals might for one reason or another work in very prestigious institutions in the first world and may well be inclined to re-read the whole of the third world from the position which is only occupied by a small number of people. I think one needs to distinguish that sort of floating postcolonialism from what I think is a long historical trend. Colonialism as I understand it is a very specific historical moment, it's the apogee of the European moment, and I think we are definitively in another moment today. This doesn't mean that we are in a moment where there is no power, no exploitation, etc, but I think one needs descriptions which are specific to the moment one is in. We are not, in that old sense, in the moment of European colonial domination anymore, which was historically very important. Also, the fact of national liberation movements and the movement of independence in the former European colonies is a very important moment. One of the things that happened is that many of the conflicts and tensions which arose from that earlier period have become what I would call internalized within those societies. Whereas the national liberation moment was a moment of freeing Algeria from France, the postcolonial moment is a moment where those tensions are operating inside, dividing one Algerian from another, and of course in relation to France—this relation hasn't gone away—and it's all taking place in relation to the global economy, which is full of neocolonization. The postcolonial is not outside of the neocolonial but it is a different moment of it. I use the notion of the postcolonial really to get at that historical specificity of what are the contradictions, what are the imbalances of power, because this is the most controversial side of it. I want to get at those specificities, because the truth is that although they are horrendous for large places around the world, like for example Africa, where I think there is just a world disaster happening, it's not easy to think of them in the old terms. What is happening in Africa is not the same as is happening in South Asia, and it is not what is happening in China either. To try to map it in the old colonial terms would be to see a European-imposed elite on top of a seethingmass of people who have other aspirations. But this is not the case any longer. The tensions are inside now, inside Iran, inside Iraq. They are all tensions left over from the other colonial moment, but now in a kind of neocolonial or postcolonial fix.

One thing you can't say about it culturally is that it is the European moment any longer. It is a moment when the West tries to hegemonize all of these situations—they try to sell them e-mail and satellites, they try to govern them, and of course, this is an activity of hegemony on the economic front and in terms of capital investment—but they aren't the only capitalists investing in this. What is most important is that in this phase, they can only move around in these societies by playing the ethnic card. They have to culturally "indigenize" themselves. They have to get into that hybrid world where Indian classical cinema meets Hollywood. They can't just impose views from outside as if there was nobody there. They are always in a kind of negotiation. I'm not utopian about this. I'm not suggesting that this is an equal game. It is a conversation of power with a lot of messes to come. But it is not the moment of *Roots*[8] any longer.

What you can hear in practically every answer to the questions you asked me is that I am trying to defend new definitions of old concepts. I want to defend identity, but in a new way; I want to defend Western culture, but in a new way; I want to be able to talk about the colonial, but in a new way. I think that's where I am. I don't want to suggest that there is a trendy postcolonial and that everything else is finished. Instead, this moment requires its own specificity of concepts, and the postcolonial gives it a kind of definition. It is the aftermath of the colonial and you can see it hovering over almost any situation you look at. It's the wake of the colonial experience, it's what has been left over as a result of that experience. And of course, it is caught in a lot of global economic processes, which are trying to reinforce it.

*Maybe a problem some people have with the notion of the postcolonial is that it sometimes appears as a new form of culturalism, where the economic level, the global economic analysis is left out of the picture. In that respect, I found what you were aiming at in your contribution to the volume on* The Post-Colonial Question[9] *very informative. Could it be the future direction of postcolonial studies to be more closely tied to the analysis of global economic processes?*

You're right, and there is a thread in your questions which does not want useful concepts to leap into a kind of culturalism which neglects the difficult issues of economic power, the inequality of power, the distribution of resources and so on—all this is perfectly correct. In part, it has to do with the disciplinary organization of knowledge. The postcolonial is very much a kind of literary discipline, which is cultural in the narrow sense. Many people working in the field talk about literature and write on literary texts, unaware about globalization, which is going on right next door, where geographers, economists and international relations people talk about the expansion of international capital. It is as if these two bodies of people haven't been introduced to each other, don't read each other's books, don't ask whether what one is saying has any purpose for what the other group is saying, or vice versa. The globalization people, too, talk on their side as if once you know the profit level, you know everything.

In that sense, I suppose it goes back to the original question you were asking me about the elite, because I do think it has been a sort of woeful neglect by many of the leading postcolonial scholars, though not all. You can't say that about Gayatri Spivak, you can't say that about Edward Said. Neither of them has ever taken postcolonialism outside the framework of cultural imperialism on the one hand, and of neo-imperialism on the other. But a large number of books pouring out about postcolonialism are as if they had never heard about the flow of international capital. So I do think that there is more work to be done, much more. I really want to explore more deeply what is at the moment not much more than a first insight into the tendency toward cultural homogenization on a global scale, the existence of local differentiation, and the fact that even when there is an inequality of power relations, nevertheless there is cultural negotiation going on.

## New Times

*Maybe we can come to the question of why conservatism has been so successful in the last twenty years. Somehow it occurs to me that what has been going on was that conservatives bought very much into the notion of cultural diversification, into all sorts of postmodernism, for instance fragmentation. They even fully bought into a kind of multiculturalist discourse, saying, "Yes, we can accept all these differences." But this was a multiculturalism that operated on a very superficial level, because it was situated on a "merely" cultural basis, while a restructuring of society associated with the notion of "New Times"*[10] *was taking place. I wonder whether the new kind of postmodern individualism, the splitting up of subjects or subjectivities into multiple subject positions doesn't go together perfectly with the restructuring of national and global economies? Maybe you can elaborate on the notion of "New Times" and how that played into the hands of neoconservatism, or was bound up with neoconservatism in the first place.*

Difficult issue, very difficult. Let me start with the thing that I least agree with and that's your view of multiculturalism …

*But this is an existing form of multiculturalist rhetoric. For instance, conservatives in Germany appreciate having Turkish cuisine around but not too many Turkish immigrants. By this, I do not mean the kind of multiculturalism that goes together with hybridity and postcolonialism. I was more thinking of a kind of political rhetoric that has established itself.*

I suppose Britain is a very particular case in this respect because the Right went along with that, but my feeling is that they're not very good on difference. They're not very good on the English-French difference, or on the English-German difference. Well, the Right didn't take up multiculturalism in its theoretical way. In Britain, the Right is very anti-theoretical in principle. They would never quote postmodernism, they regard postmodernism as a joke of the trendy intellectual Left. But your question is not about the terminology, it's whether the idea of "New Times" was grounded in anything and I think it was.

If one wanted to use such ancient terms, this is what Marx would have called the "rational core" of postmodernism. Postmodernism did genuinely see—and this might be very complicated to map—important shifts in manufacturing, from heavy industry to the service economy, all kinds of changes like that. What a broad and fantastic differentiation of the market! The market itself has become incredibly differentiated in Bourdieu's sense … and this is a very different moment of capitalism. We are not taking ourselves back to the 1920s or 1930s when everything depended on economies of scale, on mass marketing, on homogenization and standardization. This is a completely different world today, in which everything depends on marginal differences. This is a very different space altogether. And it is a space which favors greater individualism, and I think authentically that the increasing questions about identity which you asked earlier on are a by-product of that individualization, too. The less peoples' behavior, tastes, activities and life-styles can be determined collectively by the group they belong to, the more urgent is the question of identification, because you don't know how to read these people. They might look like professional middle-class, but that doesn't tell you anything about what they want, whom they vote for, what kind of life they want. There are lots of questions like these, and it is as if the mapping of collective social life has been disturbed by these changes.

I suppose the question is, was this all ideological? Was this a sort of misreading, in which case postmodernism played the unwitting game of leading us up the golden path? What I tried to do in the "New Times" thinking is to make a distinction which you might think is rather old-fashioned; in fact it is an old Marxist distinction. The point was that in certain ways, the material processes and the organization of making things and producing commodities in an advanced industrial world *do* have a certain logic to them, and I think the logic of individuation, greater individuation and greater differentiation is built into that. This would be begging a long historical question if we had a successful Soviet model, or central planning for a 150 years, but we don't have that. I'm not talking about whether we have to love the market or not, I'm talking just in terms of how things are currently produced in our world, how they are distributed and sold and used and consumed. I think there is a logic of an increasing division of labor built into that, a technological division of labor. Differentiation is the one sociological law I believe in. I think sociology is hopeless in trying to find laws, but it's the one thing that Durkheim was right about, something that Marx himself saw very early on, and Adam Smith, too. What I tried to do in *New Times* was to say that in the old world, there would have been an inevitable logic of what politics follows from this because the economy determines in the last instance, and politics and culture flow from it, but in the new world, we don't believe that any longer. The question was: Is it possible to think of a variety of political and cultural resolutions to what is in fact a kind of shift in the form of material life and its reproduction? People criticized this as sort of going back to the old base-superstructure model and I don't mean it like that, but on the other hand I've always taken the economic level quite seriously. My position on the economic is that Marx is wrong in thinking that economics determines in the *last* instance, but it certainly determines in the *first* instance, in the sense that you have to have some money to produce some goods, to hire some labor, to buy a factory, and in that sense it sets certain limits.

My argument with the Left was that Thatcherism and postmodernism are in their different ways right about a very deep and long-term historical trend in the 20th century toward individualization and differentiation. The question is: What politics can one make out of that? What culture arises as a result of that? And that's exactly my problem in relation to the Labour Party. I go with the Labour Party insofar as it wants to recognize that changed world, but I don't go with the traditional Left insofar as it pretends that we are still in the area when the trade unions where formed, when a mass industrial working class existed, and so on. I'm with Blair in the sense that this is a new world and the institutions have to reflect that, but where I'm not with him is in his capitulation exactly to the notion that if the world has changed in that way, there is only one politics left, that everybody has to have a factory—neoliberal fragmentation politics. I don't think that that's true.

In my view, Thatcherism was a deeply contradictory formation, for good reasons, because although it wanted to go with the logic of neoliberal economical-individual competitiveness, it also saw what everybody has seen since Hobbes, viz. that if you push this to the end you will have a war of all against all. There is absolutely no reason why you shouldn't push competition to the point where you eat your competitor, and at that point what everybody said was, "Now what is going to hold us together?" So they went back to the nation, to Great Britain, and to family values. Both in the United States and in Britain you see this endless attempt of circling the square between a runaway competitive individualism in the economic culture, and the question of how these communities are going to hold together, fear of crime, fear of disorganization, etc. These factors are themselves operating on both sides, and you see that there never was just a straight extrapolation from the economic neoliberal logic into culture, politics and community life. That's exactly what is terrifying the most about the Blair Labour Party—their lack of imagination. They have been unable to think of a viable but alternative way of politically taking hold of this changed world, about which they are sort of right, but not right in depth. They are sort of right about our global economy. It is perfectly true that no one nation-state can command the economic forces any longer. They are right in a broad sense talking about change, but I think they have harnessed that largely into a sort watered-down logic.

## Political Strategies

*Maybe we can move on to a related area, which is strategies of counter-hegemonic articulations, counter-hegemonic struggles. What would be the most promising strategy with respect to the politics of identity? Should it rely on discourses of identification, or should it try to expand the place where the struggle takes place? Should it take advantage of an existing party, like for instance the Labour Party, or should it try to forge completely new alliances beyond the old party system?*

If you go with what I've been saying about the break-up of many of the old social collectivities that stabilized both the Labour movement and the Conservative Party in the past, and the greater individualization and differentiation that has taken place, then you'll see that there are certain consequences with that in terms of political strategies. For one thing, you have to take a different view of the state, in two senses: one is that you are more aware of the limits of the action of the state, which is not as strong and powerful as was imagined either by the Right or by the Left. This doesn't mean that there is nothing the state can do, but it is not as strong as it was. Yet the state has also changed in another sense: whereas in the old days, one would have thought of the state as the capitalist class in power, its role is far more contradictory today. For sure, the political effectiveness of the parties organized within that system of power takes a slightly lower level today. There are going to be a lot more interesting things politically going on in civil society, in civil institutions, in social life, in the public sphere, that are not articulated in parliamentary politics. I think that this is a common phenomenon in all Western European societies. People think that politicians do not really have very much to say to them, that they lie on a number of issues, and so on. They feel how little they can do and how little you can trust them, how little what they're talking about and decide on really touches the majority. Increasingly, what touches people and what affects them is not being decided at that level. So there is a kind of shift away from the strategic sights of the old class politics.

I think the question of identification remains at the center because if your consistency for political struggles is not given by the operation of the big social collective factors, then they are much more dependent on consent. If you're not put in place by the fact that you are a manual worker, which takes your entire life, the question whether you are going to be involved in ecological questions, in community questions, or opposed to the expansion of the motor car, or opposed to out of town shopping, or opposed to a green tax etc. depends on a lot more things than what is the basis of your socio-economic wealth. For instance, it does depend on having policies and strategies, which can win an investment from you. We were right to see that the identification question is ultimately *the* political question. The political process that delivers people to issues is exactly what we don't have. There are not enough people on the right side around issues. We still haven't gained the identification investment which would allow people to support those things on a collective basis. As an old Gramscian, I'm still waiting for the moment when all these separate issues have to be negotiated. Also, political programs require difficult compromises: "Well, we won't go for this just now because that will prevent us for also going for that, and so on." I think politics does require the ability to find novel answers, the ability for genuine negotiations, which would lead to a broad coalitionist politics, even if that doesn't cohere in one political party. I'm not interested in the form so much, I'm interested in the inevitable linkages between issues, because issues don't appear separately. They don't have an impact separately. They are interconnected to one another. But there is no question that the constituted political parties play a less important role in this.

Another difficult area of strategies is the form of political institutions and movements which can have an impact globally. Many of our issues are global issues. Think about the environment. You cannot deal with it on a national basis. You cannot stop whatever is drifting across your frontier. What is the form which is capable of putting enough pressure on international corporations, which themselves have escaped the old national economic regulations and are now freewheeling in a deregulated global environment? We don't know the beginnings of that. It's full of basic contradictions, for instance what the people in the Amazon forest should live off when you're persuading them not to cut any trees. You can have beautiful rain forests, but who takes care of how they live? These contradictions are trans-national, and we don't have the agencies of a trans-national politics to tackle them. We sort of have the infrastructure, I suppose, like e-mail, travel, faxing, etc. That's very important because you can't create a constituency of movements without them, but all in all, we're very inexperienced. We're just at the beginning of a politics of that sort.

At the other end, below the level of the national, there are local communities and their need for democracy. In Britain nowadays, what we used to call democracy is practically a dirty word, because the conservatives have managed to stage a conflict between equality and democracy on the one hand and freedom on the other, and freedom is the name of the game. They don't say they're opposed to democracy, but their ordinary everyday discourse is completely anti-democratic. There are structures of power today based on national bodies that have not been elected and are not responsible to anybody. They run a huge amount of our lives now, they regulate the big authority of the republic community, they run the National Health Service that is accountable to absolutely nobody, and they spread and spread and spread. The old dream of what would happen in a mature democracy, with the capacity of ordinary people to organize their own lives, being responsible for their own communities and so on, has significantly shrunk since the 1980s and 1990s. There are all sorts of possibilities, but it's a very complicated game because it depends on linkages and articulations between different sites, operating at very different levels of organization. It is almost what people must have felt before the vote—how do you do this? How do you get people to vote? Now we think it's perfectly obvious, it has even become routinized, but I think we haven't become routinized about all these new challenges.

The one thing I don't think is that there are no issues left. What I think is in fact happening is that large areas of social life have been politicized. We have a politics of health, a politics of the body, a politics of food, a politics of sexuality, a politics of parenting, and so on. All these aspects that used to belong to the private are now being politicized from the beginning to the end. So it isn't that there aren't political issues left. It is that they don't fall neatly in place and thus be attached to political parties, to huge classes and constituencies. It is this map of the political world that we are coming out of and in a sense, are trying to put together differently.

*Let me finish with a slightly different aspect—something that also has to do with counter-hegemonic articulations but more with popular culture, or youth cultures. A lot of work you did back in the 1960s and 1970s was on youth subcultures and you developed a picture of youth subcultures as being counter hegemonic.*[11] *Is there still something to the notion of subculture that you want to hold on to? There seems to be a continuity from the 1960s until now if you just look at the strategies of putting youth cultures down, strategies of criminalization, or the Criminal Justice Act that was introduced in the early 1990s. What would you consider as the political potential of today's youth subcultures? But maybe we shouldn't call them subcultures anymore …*

Yes, I would not call them subcultures anymore. I make that qualification not because I think we were wrong to call them subcultures in the first place, but the formations are much more fleeting today and melt into one another, whereas in the 1960s, they were very distinct. Today, there is much greater fluidity in the boundaries.

Well, I don't know if I should answer that question. There is a point where one wants to stop writing about youth culture because a sort of anachronism starts creeping in, an old nostalgia with youth … but that's of course different from how to make sense of it. Suffice it to say that generation is one of the arenas that have become tremendously politicized. The speed of social change makes it obvious why that is so. Incidentally, not only between young people and adults, but also between adults and older people, these frontiers of generation and generational experience are going to be more and more important in our lives. So there is something about generation itself being constitutive of a kind of critical edge. I don't think we can say more than that. They are certainly not given as the constituencies of political and social movements. And it may well be that looking back at an underestimated number of things of what was going in the 1960s could help translate a subculture into something more than just being negatively opposed to the powers-that-be.

[1] Stuart Hall, "Cultural Studies and Its Theoretical Legacies" (1990), in David Morley, Kuan-Hsing Chen (eds.), *Stuart Hall: Critical Dialogues in Cultural Studies*. London/New York: Routledge 1996.

[2] The Centre for Contemporary Cultural Studies (CCCS) at Birmingham University, established in 1964, presided over by Stuart Hall between 1968 and 1979.

[3] Campaign for Nuclear Disarmament, British peace organization, founded in 1958.

[4] Cf. Stuart Hall, "Old and New Identities, Old and New Ethnicities," in Anthony King (ed.), *Culture, Globalization and the World*. London: Macmillan 1991.

[5] Sheila Rowbotham, Lynne Segal, Hilary Wainwright, *Beyond the Fragments: Feminism and the Making of Socialism*. London: The Merlin Press Ltd. 1979.

[6] Cf. Stuart Hall, "The Problem of Ideology: Marxism without Guarantees" (1983), in David Morley, Kuan-Hsing Chen (eds.), *Stuart Hall: Critical Dialogues in Cultural Studies*; cf. also Paul Gilroy, Lawrence Grossberg, Angela McRobbie (eds.), *Without Guarantees: In Honour of Stuart Hall*. London/New York: Verso 2000.

[7] Quoted in David Morley, Kuan-Hsing Chen (eds.), "Introduction," in *Stuart Hall: Critical Dialogues in Cultural Studies*, p. 15.

[8] Famous television dramatization of Alex Hailey's slavery novel, directed by Marvin J. Chomsky and others, released in 1977.

[9] Stuart Hall, "When Was 'the Post-Colonial?' Thinking at the Limit," in Iain Chambers, Lidia Curti (eds.), *The Post-Colonial Question: Common Skies, Divided Horizons*. London/New York: Routledge 1996.

[10] Stuart Hall, Martin Jacques (eds.), *New Times: Changing Face of Politics in the 1990s*. London: Lawrence & Wishart Ltd. 1989; see also Stuart Hall, *The Hard Road to Renewal: Thatcherism and the Crisis of the Left*. London: Verso 1988.

[11] Cf. Stuart Hall, Tony Jefferson (eds.), *Resistance through Rituals: Youth Subcultures in Post-War Britain*. Birmingham: CCCS 1976 (Reprint: London/New York: Routledge 1993).

# *Lines of Flight, Exits Closed*
# Conversation with Lawrence Grossberg

Interview conducted in April 1996.

What political potential does popular culture contain? In what ways does it encourage the withdrawal into private life? What forms of resistance are there to combat the prevailing ideology of ironic cynicism? Lawrence Grossberg, a pioneering Cultural Studies apologist and "rock 'n' roll professor," strikes some dissonant chords regarding the deregulation of the former public sphere, the re-regulation of everyday life, and the success of the New Right.

Lawrence Grossberg became well-known through the publication of the massive Routledge *Cultural Studies Reader.** But he has also produced notable theoretical works of his own. Best-known among these is his book *We Gotta Get Out of This Place,*** in which he examined the connection between American neoconservatism and pop culture. Grossberg traces the path of the counterculture of the 1960s to the political and marketing strategies of the 1990s, a decade in which the dilemma of failing authenticity vs. facetious cynicism became more apparent than ever before. In this situation, there seem to be no emergency exits in sight, and they are certainly not to be found in an insistence on difference driven by identity politics. Escape routes from everyday life may indeed be blocked, but according to Grossberg, it is still the pop area and in particular new musical formations that make it bearable to endure this despotic machine called capitalism.

* Lawrence Grossberg, Cary Nelson, Paula Treichler (eds.), *Cultural Studies*. New York/London: Routledge 1992.

** Lawrence Grossberg, *We Gotta Get Out of This Place: Popular Conservatism and Postmodern Culture*. New York/London: Routledge 1992.

CH *The argument you laid out in your book* We Gotta Get Out of This Place *was primarily concerned with neoconservatism as it re-emerged in the United States in the 1980s. Your claim is that this re-emergence was crucially enacted through culture. If I understood you correctly, you argue that, while there has been an increasing liberalization and deregulation in the field of economics, the cultural sphere has become increasingly regulated. Can you explain what exact role culture plays within neoconservatism? Why is it that culture has become this kind of battlefield against, let's say, the political sphere or economic sphere?*

LG One of the interesting things about the global success of neoconservatism—and I very much agree with Stuart Hall in this respect—is that this is a political position in which people are supporting the conservatives even though they do not agree with their ideology. Stuart Hall gives an analysis of how that was effected in Britain by the struggle over what he calls common sense.

That was not how it was working in America, though. The struggle for people's hearts in America was carried out not by trying to change the ways they interpreted the world, but by trying to change the ways they felt about the world. It is what I call "affective"—and I'm not sure if that's true anywhere else. There is a famous interview with one of the leaders of the neoconservatives, Bill Buckley. When he was asked about the success of neoconservatism, he said, "We read a lot of economic and political theory and developed our agenda; then we read a lot of cultural theory and developed our strategy." What they did was really to figure out that the biggest changes in American society since the Second World War had been largely propelled through popular culture. The 1960s revolution, for example, was not a revolution of economics or politics but a revolution which operated through popular culture by changing people's feelings and everyday lives: the behavior, the ways they talked and walked. The neocons realized that what they had to do was to use that same strategy, now against the 1960s. I think one of the ironies is that these are people who grew up on rock 'n' roll, understood it very well and finally turned it against itself. They used the powerful appeal of rock 'n' roll to emotions and the body in order to change the ways in which people live their lives. They've been very successful with this and still are, which is very frightening. My book suggests—although I did not argue this explicitly—that even Bill Clinton's victory was a clear victory for the conservatives, because Clinton, who has been constructed as a liberal, is clearly a kind of conservative. Behind all of this, I think, is capitalism and the deregulation of the market—the creation of what Gilles Deleuze called a *despotic market* that controls everything. While this despotic market is deregulating itself, it is re-regulating everything else in the name of capital.

*You have already touched upon my second question, which is how the so-called "rock formation"—which was built up from the 1950s onwards and which reached its peak in the 1960s—exactly figures within neoconservatism. The latter seems to have an ambivalent relation toward rock 'n' roll culture: on the one hand, there are all sorts of attacks and even attempts at censorship; on the other hand, as you claimed, neoconservatives used it and appropriated countercultural strategies of the 1960s. How do these two things go together?*

If you think of rock 'n' roll as a mode of communication, a mode of communication that is not so much worried about communicating meaning or information, about representing the world or ideology, but rather as a mode of communication that can create and organize feelings as well as energy, then this mode of communication can also be employed to construct systems of differences—"us and them," people who are part of rock 'n' roll culture and people who are not. In this respect, it can be designed around the changing of everyday life as opposed to struggling over political issues. I think what the New Right really did was to say, "We are going to use that mode of communication for exactly the opposite ends." In some ways, and I can't decide whether this is consciously or unconsciously so, they really *do* understand what they are doing. I discovered after the book was written that the Republicans, as one embodiment of the New Right, developed their campaign strategy through a new technique where they test slogans by measuring peoples' galvanomic skin responses. What galvanomic measurement does is it to test the immediate unconscious emotional response. They show people slogans like "A thousand points of lights" and they measure their emotional responses to it. Then, they pick those slogans that get the highest emotional responses. There was an interview with the guy who had invented this technique in which they said to him, "But you don't know how people interpret these slogans," and he said, "We don't care. We don't want them to understand the slogans. Meaning only gets in the way. We want them to respond immediately. It is almost like a rhythm we want. Just like people move their bodies to a rhythm, we want peoples' bodies to move to a slogan. We don't want them to think about the content, we don't want them to ask what 'A thousand points of lights' means, we just want them to feel the rhythm." That is how they developed their campaign strategy. It seems to me the best sort of way to describe how rock 'n' roll was created.

*Doesn't this picture suggest that popular culture only operates on a purely affective level? Doesn't it also have a huge intentional dimension?*

Certainly, popular culture in general operates not only on an affective level but also ideologically, semantically, and cognitively. I think one of the interesting things about music is that in music the emotional, the affective, and the shared energy often overwhelms its ideological dimension. Increasingly, what has happened in rock 'n' roll is that this overwhelming ability has become almost total. An interesting thing about the 1980s—I'm not sure about the 1990s—was that you got a lot of music that was political again. After the 1970s, when music like disco and pop, not to speak about punk, was incredibly depoliticized, mainstream music became quite political again in the 1980s. You got musicians like Sting, who was doing all sorts of political things, you got Tracy Chapman singing about the need for a "revolution," and you got bands like Midnight Oil. However, as far as I can tell the kids just ignored the politics. When Midnight Oil played in the city in Illinois where I was teaching at that time, all the reviews of their concerts said, "This is the greatest rock 'n' roll band of the country, but their politics are kind of boring—who cares?" And it was an extraordinary ability to just ignore the ideological aspect of it.

*Something similar seemed to happen when rap and hip-hop were appropriated by white kids …*

I don't think so. I think that there is increasingly a kind of desperate identification of white and black kids. In the 1950s, the 1960s, and the 1970s, white kids wanted to pretend that they were like black kids. I think in the 1990s white kids think they *are* black. And in some ways they really are, if you just look at the context of growing up being young in America, economically, in terms of what their future is, in terms of how the legal system is treating them, in terms of all of their rights being taken away. I think white kids feel more and more that they are functionally black and there is at least a possibility of identification. One of the problems is that instead of encouraging this identification, Left critics ignore it, attack rap, talk about cooptation and selling out, instead of saying, "Right on, you are black!" We are not helping white kids to find new ways of imagining their relationship to the music, we're not coming back and saying, "Yes, maybe this is what you're feeling." We're criticizing them.

*I was thinking about when white people like us listen to some of the more aggressive gangsta rap. While you can easily enjoy the rhythm, you have to ignore all the sexist and homophobic dimensions.*

Well, you have to ignore it in most rock 'n' roll. The Rolling Stones were homophobic and sexist, and a lot of punk was sexist and racist and homophobic.

*But nowadays, there is much more consciousness about those aspects …*

Today, there is a lot of dialogue taking place within the rap community, and there are debates around these issues. Also, figuring out the meaning of the kind of sexism in rap is a complex problem. If you think about the black community and the relationships within it, I think we need to be criticizing those kinds of things, but we also need to give these rappers and the communities that identify with them a way out. Not just tell them that their entire investment in rap is politically suspect because of this. I can remember having all these debates in the 1970s and 1980s with kids listening to heavy metal because this music was so sexist, racist and homophobic. What kids would often tell you was, "We don't care about that, that's not why we like it. It would be nice if it wasn't that way but we like it for other reasons and those other reasons are much more important to us." Obviously, there was, and probably still is, a part of the heavy metal audience that is invested in racism, sexism, and homophobia, just as there is a part of the black community that is invested in homophobia. We need to struggle against that, but we also need to realize that that's not why they are listening to rap. It's not the homophobia that is bringing them to rap. It is the anger, it is a sense that they're getting screwed, that life really is getting harder and harder, instead of getting better and better. Rap is the only place where there is that sense of anger—a sense of energy and agency that's coming out for young black kids. So once again, I think the Left is failing kids in terms of trying to help them find ways to make sense of what their lives are like.

*Coming back to the strategies of neoconservatism, you outline three basic trajectories:* the appropriation of the postmodern frontier, *creating an* affective epidemics, *and finally, what I want to talk about more extensively here, a strategy you call* disciplined mobilization. *Can you explain what you mean by it?*

It basically means two things. First, it seems to me that, instead of marginalizing or repressing in public those on the outside, there is an erasure of the presence of people who are not middle class. A literal enforcement of discipline is taking place. One example that has only come to light recently is this drug called Ritalin. It is a very odd drug, a kind of "speed," but when you give it to hyperactive children, it works as a tranquilizer. Nowadays, it is administered to about ten million kids in the United States. Kids who have been diagnosed with what they call Attention Deficit Syndrome are given Ritalin. As far as I can tell, these kids are just bored. They act out their boredom at school but instead of dealing with that, what the authorities do is erase them by giving them a drug that makes them enact their boredom in a disciplined way. From what I can tell, we were all suffering of Attention Deficit Syndrome in public school. We were all bored and hyperactive but now, instead of just oppressing them, what we do is discipline them with drugs that make them act like good middle-class kids are supposed to act. So part of "disciplined mobilization" is to literally erase the homeless, not even putting them in jail, but putting them entirely out of the sphere of visibility.

The second aspect concerns the fact that America has always had a real commitment to the ideology of mobility and this notion of being mobile kind of gave America its sense of optimism. What has happened recently is that mobility continues to be the dominant ideology, but instead of mobility being defined as a movement up, it's just fine as long as you move. As long as you keep moving in your everyday life, your economic life, etc., it's ok. There is this odd sense in which the normal path of American economics is that people move up and down, you lose your job, you get another. It does not seem to bother people that this is happening, because it's the movement itself that suggests that society is in good shape. I haven't really thought about this, but the kind of emphasis in techno on this incredible sense of movement and speed seems to suggest the same kind of thing. The metaphor I use is that for a while before Reagan, there was this kind of Foucaultian image of discipline: that you were getting into your car and your car was instantly measuring your alcohol level—because there is a big scare about drunk driving in America—and it would transmit that information to the police, and they would come and arrest you. But nowadays I think the metaphor is more like: you're getting into your car, the car measures your alcohol level and tells you, "You can't drive." The state doesn't need to be involved, because it's now anchored in everyday life that you can or cannot do things. That you can't go here or there. The segregation between black and white is not an institutional segregation, but it is a voluntary segregation in everyday life. It's not political or economic anymore, but it's a willful choice about one's everyday behavior that seems to create an organization of power. It's something like that that I have in mind and I'm still trying to theorize it. I might need to think more about ideas like possibility and how to regulate possibility (as suggested by philosophers like Deleuze) in order to describe it.

## The Private and the Ironic

*Something that has certainly taken place is a tendency toward the privatization of previously public concerns, a return to the private, an increased focus on private life that maybe started out with the realization that there is not much you can effectively do in a public arena. Would you conceive of this tendency just as an increased post-modern fragmentation and individualization, or is there something more to it?*

One of the things I want to get at with the notion of disciplined mobilization is that the distinction between the public and the private has broken down. People are often too easily convinced that the New Right is deregulating the public realm and re-regulating the private. But if you think about it that way it doesn't really work, because nowadays the distinction has to be understood between everyday life and, let's call it something like institutional life. What is increasingly happening is a deregulation of institutions *as* individuals because in America, institutions and corporations have the rights of individuals. So in an odd sense, that realm is included in the private. Corporations have the right of privacy because they are granted the rights of individuals. What is being re-regulated is something that I want to call everyday life, in Lefebvre's sense, which is mostly public.

It has to do with education: while schools are being deregulated, life in schools is being re-regulated; while museums are being deregulated, the actual practice of museums is being re-regulated. I think it is the distinction between everyday life and something else, the institutional, but I'm not sure that that's the best description of it, that is at stake here.

*In the 1970s, the famous feminist slogan was that "the personal is political." You were rethinking this in terms of developments during the 1980s, coming to the result that nowadays, "the personal is the only political." If privacy and the public sphere have collapsed and everything has become a part of everyday life, can there still be a place for the political somewhere?*

Well, I still think that there is a politics of everyday life. I think of it as disciplined mobilization instead of institutions, and in my book I talk about it as the conditions of possibility of everyday life. It is precisely our inability to think about the conditions that are constituting everyday life in the forms it has that makes it so hard to struggle against them. And while it is important to struggle over the patterns of everyday life, we are going to fail unless we begin to challenge the conditions that are organizing public life, because it is those larger struggles that are at stake. In the US, there is a kind of ecology movement in everyday life but none is taking place in "official" America. There are a lot of people talking about it, and there are local struggles, but unless we can organize a national struggle against the conditions of the possibility of environmental disaster, we will not be able to stop it. Bill Clinton is talking about raising the minimum wage, which is a struggle within everyday life, but what we really have to do is to change the corporate tax structure in America, which is the major economic source of the disaster of the American economy: that is, if corporations in America were paying taxes at the rates they paid in the 1950s we would not have any debts, and if we made them start to pay those taxes again we could eliminate all debts in under a decade. Those are the conditions of possibility of what is going on in everyday life, but no one is talking about the corporate tax structure except the Republicans, who want to make it even easier for corporations. We argue about middle-class tax breaks, but not about the conditions of possibility of those tax breaks which have to do with the larger tax structure and their relationships to corporate profit and corporate growth, and to economic indicators which are increasingly geared not toward everyday life, as they were in the 1950s, but to measurements of corporate profitability.

*But viewed from an individual level, from the level of taxpayers, or people involved in popular culture, there is certainly a form of de-politicization that has taken place. This process is not only about increasing fragmentation, or that there is no forum for public organization anymore. It's rather what Deleuze has called "lines of flight" that have become more and more regulated.*

There is a big segment of the Left in America that is talking about the "public sphere" in some re-reading of Jürgen Habermas. But I don't believe that the problem is the collapse of the "public sphere," because there are significant problems prior to that. I think what the Right has done is to challenge the necessary conditions of political struggle. In order to have political struggle you need to have people caring about politics, which means that they do not only care about their own everyday life but about larger structures. You need to have a faith, you need to have models of community and alliance for politics, and you need to have a faith in agency. You need to have models of how one can intervene in the political process. I think the Right has capitalized and mobilized a kind of de-politicization, a kind of apathy in which we no longer have any ability to invest ourselves in politics. We no longer have any model of alliance and we no longer have any notion of strategic agency. Unless we can find ways of challenging that, unless we can get people to reinvest in political struggle, to re-imagine alliance and re-conceptualize what agency means in the contemporary global political sphere, it doesn't matter if you have a "public sphere." It doesn't matter if I stand up and say, "If we just changed the corporate tax structure, we would be better off." If we can't figure out how to get blacks and gays and women and ecologists to sit down and say, "Okay, let's struggle over that together." And if we can't get people to care!

I think the problem is very deep in America, and it may be similar in the rest of the world, but I don't know what it's like in the rest of the world, probably because the nature of American culture is not to care about the rest of the world, which is of course part of the problem. We don't care about the rest of the world, which is also a part of not caring about the political, because in order to understand politics and economics in the contemporary world you have to look at global relations. But part of what the Right has done is to create a kind of disinvestment from the global, so suddenly people in America accept the argument that the only reason we should become involved in a dispute somewhere else in the world is because of American interests. That becomes a very personalized relationship to the political which we need to challenge. We need to understand that we shouldn't be invested in the rest of the world because it's our interest or because we're the moral police of the world, but because we are interested in political struggle and we are interested in changing America. In order to change America, the society of America, we need to consider the fact that politics and economics are now global. We are already involved and invested in the Persian Gulf and we are already involved and invested everywhere in the world. We should be acting in ways that are thought of politically in more sophisticated and passionate ways.

*Talking about the apathy that plays a vital role in neoconservatism, doesn't this go together well with the huge amount of cynicism and irony that is also almost like an everyday condition today, an everyday mood? You have it everywhere, from talk shows to the ways in which individuals think about political things, almost like a particular kind of postmodern sensibility. Can you talk about how such postmodern sensibilities like irony or the grotesque figure in the neoconservative backlash?*

I think that in a sense the two are equivalent. The structure of apathy is being produced, in part, by the New Right, but it is broader than that. I think the New Right is simply taking advantage of things that are happening in a wider context. The New Right is articulating a kind of ironic cynicism into a political apathy so that for instance you are not only cynical about the possibilities of investing in politics or about possibilities of changing the world, but you then become ironic about that impossibility so that you don't have to feel bad about your cynicism. People are often cynical, but part of this cynicism is a kind of structure of inadequacy, of lack. To say, "Well, I'm cynical" is to say there must have been a time when I wasn't cynical and there will be a time when I won't be cynical. But if you can be ironic about your cynicism, then cynicism becomes the kind of dominant trope and there doesn't have to be any imagination of something that's not cynical. I think American culture has become increasingly predicated on this odd, almost oxymoronic combination, viz. that nothing is going to change and even if it did change, it would just get worse, and if you could get it better, someone else would co-opt it to their own selfish ends, and then to kind of laugh at that! A telling example of this kind of hypocrisy is the so-called war on drugs. Everybody realizes that it's hypocritical and they kind of shrug it off and laugh and say, "Well, yes, it's kind of hypocritical." I'm not quite sure where that comes from, but its latest manifestation, which is the most frightening, is what I'm beginning to call the celebration of stupidity in America. Some of the most successful movies in America today are films like *Forrest Gump*, *Dumb and Dumber* or the *Beavis & Butthead* shows. The only models of public life that become popular are models of absolute stupidity. In *Forrest Gump*, it is a model of stupidity that is the only path to success because everyone else in the movie fails! In a sense, the stupidity in *Beavis & Butthead* or *The Simpsons* becomes a new source of heroicism, but in fact, it is an extraordinarily disabling strategy. Of course, the Right knows that they are not going to stop it so they can both criticize it and use it. They can criticize these movies for being immoral and at the same time, they can build on the fact that stupidity is becoming a celebrated feature in America.

*Within this whole wave of cynicism, aren't people also, on a kind of meta-level, laughing about their own inability to move anywhere, as if they are stuck in life and the only thing they can do about it is laugh?*

I think the irony is partly predicated on the fact that we know or *can* know everything. The internet just makes that worse. There is such a surplus of information today that you can know everything and as a result, you don't know anything. There is so much information out there, so many interpretations, you're so overwhelmed by it that what you have to do is retreat from it and not know anything. So in the face of the fact that you could get on the internet and get information about anything in the world—and you can probably get better news than on the news networks in America—you retreat because it's just impossible to cope with it anymore. I actually think my generation, the baby boomers of the post-World War years, were responsible for it, because we were a generation that was the first generation to have access to knowing about anything. Television brought us into places that we had never been in before, our parents' bedroom, Congress ... you could see what you had never been seeing before, but the result is that you retreat from it and create a false illusion that you don't know what is going on when in fact, of course you do, all you have to do is look. And you're constantly looking but you deny the look, you deny that you know it. The Republicans with all their talk about the family should have a look at what's happening to the family. America has one of the highest poverty rates among children in the world and it's in the news all the times. *The New York Times* had a big headline when the Republicans proposed their welfare reform that said that ten million children would slip into poverty as a result. But what do Americans do? They just sort of deny it and support the Republicans, support the idea that welfare mothers are a pain in the ass. It is a very odd sense in which stupidity becomes willful as an escape from cynicism, an escape from the information which you can't cope with.

Again, I don't know how to get out of that, because these developments are not simply a political strategy. It is cultural tendencies which are being used and articulated as a political strategy and unless we can find ways to take those same strategies, those same tendencies and develop new articulations, new ways of using them to more progressive ends, we aren't going to be able to battle them. We can't hold on to moral purity and attack people for being ignorant in the face of *Forrest Gump*. Because people don't want to be given more information about what's going on in the world. They want to escape from the fact that they already have too much information and they can't figure out what to do about it. You can't keep hitting them over the head in the name of truth. You have to find some way of taking *Forrest Gump* and saying, "This is how you feel, maybe here is an alternative political strategy that we can work out together and that wouldn't end up where the Republicans want us to end up or where Clinton wants us to end up."

*Maybe we can come back to the "rock formation" now, or to more concrete examples of popular culture. You are claiming that rock 'n' roll, like music generally, works both as a "territorializing machine" and as a "differentiating machine." I briefly wanted to ask you how exactly one has to conceive of the relation between the two aspects?*

That's a hard question ...

*Part of your argument is that during the 1980s the differentiating machine seems to have collapsed. Couldn't one also say that now there are so many differences existing simultaneously on the market that it doesn't matter anymore, at least politically, what you listen to, or what you affiliate yourself with musically?*

In fact, I have an article called "Is anybody listening? Does anybody care?" (1994),[1] which basically argues that the rock formation as I described it, as a differentiation and territorializing machine, is dead, that it no longer exists. Today, I'm going to pull back a little and say it still exists but it's a kind of residual or marginal part of popular culture and that the most interesting developments in popular music are a new kind of mainstream formation. This new mainstream is radically eclectic and has no differentiating function whatsoever. Within this formation, people are much more tolerant of other people's tastes, so instead of the old rock 'n' roll strategy of saying, "You don't like my music, you don't understand rock 'n' roll," or "You're listening to disco, you don't understand rock 'n' roll," people are more like "Oh that's cool, you like disco." At the same time, they also have much more eclectic tastes. I ask my students every year what their favorite records are and I am amazed at the increasing leaps in genre. Their favorite records would be Nine Inch Nails *and* Janet Jackson, putting together categories that one would have thought of as exclusive. That's a fairly new kind of relationship to music, and it is connected partly to the fact that, as Simon Frith has argued, people's relationship to music is increasingly not so much about the music anymore, but the things you can do with the music. As Simon put it, in the 1990s you don't dance to the music you like, but you like the music you can dance to. Dance becomes more important than the music and you like whatever music you can dance to. You don't pick friends who like the same music as you do, but you like the music your friends listen to. I spent last summer hanging out with a group of high school students, going to their parties and it was amazing because they would go from Nine Inch Nails to Garth Brooks to Coolio. They would just mix everything up and they would dance to all that and when I asked about it they said, "What's important isn't the music, it's about us getting together as group of friends, it's about having a good time, it's about dancing, it's about all these other things, not about what we actually like in the music." We can dance to Garth Brooks, we have fun line dancing, so we listen to Garth Brooks, we have fun dancing to rap, we have fun teasing each other about this and that." It seems to me that that's a very different relationship to music.

*So there is not really any style war going on anymore?*

Not in that group. There is a kind of residual group which holds on to that old ideology of rock 'n' roll, a kind of alternative, which still believes it's authentic and the rest is all sold out. But I also think that there is a third formation, which I don't quite understand yet, a third form of popular music which is organized around geographies, scenes, and a lot of it has to do with dance music. I don't understand it because I'm not very involved in dance music. The music you hear in Manchester or New York is different from the usual rock scene, the dance scenes are different. They may have relations but they are different, they each have their own sense of identity. And they each have a sense of geographical loyalty and that exists as well in the rock scene, in the sense that Chapel Hill for instance has a scene. What happens is that as soon as record companies get involved you get a Seattle scene been marketed as grunge. But if you go to Seattle and talk to Seattle fans, they'll tell you grunge is only one of the parts of the Seattle scene. There are lots of stylistic things going on in Seattle. But there is a kind of scene in Seattle and the loyalty is to Seattle. You get people moving to Seattle because they want to be part of that scene. The same is true in Chapel Hill. When there isn't a Chapel Hill sound, there is a kind of Chapel Hill scene and people are enormously loyal to that scene, which isn't generic. It's not like "We like alternative as opposed to ...," because the Chapel Hill scene includes rap and all sorts of dance. It includes all these different things and people are committed to the scene, and I think we haven't had that before. That's a new way of being related to music. In a way, it is differentiating because it is based on a principle like, "I'm in the Chapel Hill scene and not in the Seattle Scene or the Austin scene." You have a real loyalty and you get arguments about which is the better scene, Chapel Hill, or Seattle, or Austin, or Atlanta. You get people coming to the scene, you get bands moving because they want to be part of a particular scene. You get fans moving because they like a special scene. It's a very interesting kind of organization and in a way, it's also radically territorializing because it's so spatial. It literally involves inventing geographical places in which a wide variety of things can happen, but not everything. The Chapel Hill scene has almost no grunge. There are one or two grunge bands but it is a very minor part of that scene.

One interesting thing is that so many rock critics and so many academic rock people are so invested in what I would now call the "residual formation," but no one is really studying either the new eclectic mainstream or this new kind of organization of rock around scenes.[2] When you write about scenes, what you end up writing about is the marketing of scenes—how Seattle is being marketed as the grunge scene and Austin as the rhythm and blues centre—and not the actual territorializing of a place. This is interesting, because in the face of globalization, place becomes increasingly important. A sense of the local becomes increasingly relevant and I see that happening now in a lot of music. My friends are invested in the New York dance scene but not in dance generally. It's the New York dance scene they go to, they don't like to go to London. The London dance scene is different.

*The Detroit dance scene being something different again ...*

And no one is really studying it, no one is writing about it. No one is thinking about the political significance of it. The politics of authenticity that defined rock, they are easily recognizable, but what are the politics of eclecticism? And what are the politics of geographical scenes and how could they offer a way to counter the New Right? Do they offer new logics of popular culture which might be a weapon against ironic cynicism? Authenticity has become ironic cynicism for most people, but does this offer a way out of ironic cynicism, because now something does matter again? Either the kind of liberal tolerance of eclecticism, or the sense of identity that comes from place.[3] Of course, as we know from Serbia, a sense of place as the basis of an investment can be very dangerous. So what are the possibilities of these new emergent organizations of popular music? I'm just beginning to think about those. I'm trying to be optimistic about them, to say that maybe they allow us to think of a new way of fighting because it was the ideology of authenticity that later became the ideology of ironic cynicism. So does the ideology of eclecticism, of territorializing without differentiating, or of differentiating geographically by place, does that offer an answer to ironic cynicism? Are these kids searching for ways of caring for themselves, for their lives, their friends and their future that isn't based on mythologies of authenticity and rebellion?

*Still, the basic question is how somewhere in this setting a new outside, or new lines of flight, could emerge. Your argument was that, within the strategy of de-territorialization that slowly became the new territorialization machine, everything outside has been erased. My question is: Has there really ever been an outside within the rock formation? And is there any possibility that a new outside can be created through those local scenes, the new geographic structuring of the music scene? Or, to put in another way: Wasn't rock's power always more disruptive than creative? Didn't it have more a negating force toward existing society rather than creating a positive vision of an outside?*

It always had a positive side to it, but I don't think rock was ever political in the strict ideological sense. Rock was always sexist, it was always racist and I think the mythology that rock somehow challenged the dominant ideology was created by rock fans as they grew up and became political and wanted to legitimate their own taste. I do think that at moments, rock has had an outside, like in the 1960s, but that was accidental and selfish. In the late 1960s counterculture, the outside, existed as our personal ability to have an inside was suddenly threatened. The draft and Vietnam became such an outside impinged upon us. But I think rock in general never engaged with the outside, it always acknowledged the outside, it always kind of protected itself from it and acknowledged that the outside was there and had to draw a line so that it didn't have to confront it. I think that by the 1980s it forgot about it; the outside just disappeared. I think that bands like Gang of Four—and that is my desperate optimism if I want—were political, but on the inside. It was all about the politics of everyday life. You had bands like The Clash that seemed to be talking about the outside, but they were so vague and again, so easily ignored, that I don't think it was a real politics. There were bands like Crass, punk heroes who aimed at that, but no one took them seriously. Crass seems to have disappeared from the histories of punk altogether. But I wonder if today, there isn't an outside for the kids again. Michel de Certeau has this idea that he calls—and I have no idea where it comes from—a "polemological" politics. A polemological politics is a discourse that says, "We're getting fucked and we know who is doing it to us—it is you!" One of the interesting things about rap is that it has that attitude, "We're getting fucked and we know who is doing it. We know it's the cops, we know it's capitalism, we know it's the government, we know it's the white man and we'll name that." That's where my optimism comes in, about white kids listening to rap. I wonder whether around rap there isn't a possibility of a new kind of politics in which kids are now really starting off by saying, "We're getting fucked," and they are, whereas in the 1950s rock started off by saying, "We're bored ... we're bored and we want to have fun." But in the 1990s, it's very different. The kids are not bored, because they got the music, they can have fun. The problem is that they don't know what is going to happen in the future, because they know that society is out to screw them. Society doesn't care about them. But again, the problem is what will happen if they continue to get screwed. Unless we can find a way to take that popular politics and connect it to some kind of political struggle that doesn't dismiss their feelings, that doesn't dismiss their anger, as contradictory as it may be, as sexist as it may be, as homophobic as it may be, but that takes it seriously and finds a way of connecting it to something beyond identity, something beyond anger, it's just going to continue to exist without any real ability to struggle against the outside.[4]

*This brings me to my last point, which is about new strategies for the Left or for oppositional politics in general. What you criticize very harshly is all the investments in a politics of identity that is more or less a differentiating machine working on the political level. What would you consider the most promising strategy for achieving an oppositional hegemony, or challenging the dominating hegemonic block?*

If I knew that I could run for president!

*I mean, it cannot just take place on the level of everyday life, it cannot be an investment in marginality …*

Well, it has to start from the majority of people's very real fears and hopes. People are afraid of immigrants in America taking their jobs, they are afraid of what affirmative action programs have done to their future, they are afraid of the moral collapse of America, and all that means that we have to start there. We have to find ways of saying, "Well yes, morality is a problem." The Left in America is oddly contradictory because on the one hand, it thinks it's morally correct, while on the other hand, it refuses to talk about morality because it thinks morality is a right-wing issue. But we need not assume that we know the morality. We need to speak to the fact that people are worried about the lack of it, what they perceive as a lack of morality in America. We need to address the fact that people are upset about crime, and if you look at the statistics in America, you will notice that crime is not entirely black. It has certainly been constructed as entirely black, and it is significantly but not exclusively black. We need to address that concern but not allow it to become racism. We can't ignore the fact that the Right is taking people's feelings and connecting them to real political struggles. We need to go back and ask what people are feeling, and what we can do with them without assuming that we know what they should be feeling or that their feelings are inherently conservative or inherently wrong. At the same time, we need to accept that people are flawed. One of the problems the Left has is that it spends so much time attacking *itself*—"Their political position is racist." We need to be able to say, "Well okay, your political position may be flawed, you may not be the most perfect human being, but you are an ally and even if you don't agree with me on everything we can work together to begin to make some changes." And then as we're working through those changes on what we agree upon we can work through the things we disagree upon, instead of needing to agree ahead of time. "I can't support you because I think you're homophobic, but you're maybe anti-racist, anti-sexist, anti-capitalist, so let's start because we can put together a coalition on those issues. And as we're gaining success we'll start to address the homophobic question. But if we're going to say ahead of time that we're not going to work with anyone who is homophobic, we're not going to work with anyone who is pro-capitalist, we're just never going to get enough people together who agree on anything." One of the interesting things in America is all this talk about left-wing third parties because the Democrats have become conservative. But instead of getting together and saying, "Well, what can we agree upon as the basis of a third party?" what we now have are four different left-wing third parties. One says ecology, the second one say capitalism and labor, the third says race, and so on, instead of just saying, "Let's get together and find the common ground that we have, let's find out where we agree in order to begin working."

*Maybe there is no common ground for all of these.*

Maybe, and then we have to deal with that, but unless you start to try …

*Viewed in a negative way, if you distance yourself from the hegemonic block, there might be something like a common ground …*

But it can't be negative, it has to be positive. But that has to be made! It's not that the common ground is already there. The common ground may come by sitting at a table and holding each other there even when you want to leave. It seems to me that that's part of the lesson of Ernesto Laclau and Chantal Mouffe that no one takes seriously, that articulations have to be *made*, that they cannot be taken for granted. That means that you have to sit the ecologists down with the black and anti-racist activists, and even though they may want to kill each other, you have to hold them back and say, "Let's reach a point where we have some common ground and start the struggle there. And then as we go on we may find broader and broader areas of struggle. The articulations will change *us* as we work, instead of this kind of demand that the agenda be all set." It seems to me that for all of the work that has been done in the past fifty years on the notions of cultural politics, cultural struggle, and articulation, and despite the fact that everyone reads Gramsci on hegemony, Laclau/Mouffe on articulation and Foucault on discourse, we don't seem to take articulation seriously. We don't seem to take seriously the fact that discourse actually *has* effects and that discursive work *is* important. We don't seem to take seriously the fact that hegemony is an ongoing struggle that needs to be continuously re-conceptualized, redefined, remade, etc. It seems to me that unless we start taking seriously the things we've being saying for the past thirty years, we can't begin to challenge the Right.

*One last question: How do you think popular culture or music can figure in this new struggle for alliances, or in the building of a common ground? If everything is radically split up, into geographically particular sites as you outlined before, won't it be very difficult to articulate, to make articulations among all those different scenes?*

It seems to me that popular culture has to play a crucial role because in general, popular culture is where people's feelings, hopes, and desires are articulated, constructed, and interpreted. Unless we take popular culture seriously and work in it in order to *remake* popular culture, we can't speak to those feelings and desires. We need not only to take *Forrest Gump* seriously and ask what it means that people like this stuff, but we need to make our own *Forrest Gumps*, with slightly different endings. Popular music is also going to be crucial, for two reasons: The first one is obvious, because if we're going to do this we need to win young people to our side; and one of the problems the Left has is that it keeps telling young people that they're conservative, or that they're racist, or that they're homophobic. Hence they keep saying, "Well, so we're conservatives then. We don't want to listen to you." We need to start talking to these kids again, through their music, about their music, and in ways that don't alienate them.

The second thing is that American youth are a wonderfully potential site to organize political struggle. It is the place where the new conservatism is the most challenging, and probably the easiest to challenge. We are really screwing over the kids, in all the ways we have talked about, in terms of their future but also in terms of how they're living. Considering the consequences of the current economic changes on kids' lives, the consequences of Republican and Democratic strategies on education and child welfare, and recognizing the kind of emotional appeal that notions of family and childhood have in America, the popularity of people like Steven Spielberg or Robin Williams, with their ability to mobilize images of childhood, could make a difference in realizing that that's a very important articulatory point in American politics. But in order to achieve that goal we need to be working with kids so that they don't feel we're exploiting them for our own purposes. If the Republicans are, why shouldn't we be working with kids, why shouldn't we be talking with them? Finally, I do believe that music is a powerful form of culture and that it really is the site in which you can work affectively and emotionally with people. Since it has been such an important player in the cultural and political field over the past fifty years, it will most likely continue to be so.

What we need to do is give up the residual model of marginality and authenticity and we need to move on to these other models of scenes, of geographical scenes and of mainstream eclecticism, and ask what possibilities they have. The interesting thing about scenes, although it is a different kind of differentiating machine, is that it is not a binary one. It's not "us and them." There are scenes that make connections and scenes that support each other, so for instance, you get dance networks. There are ways in which the scenes are articulated with each other. We need to think about that as a kind of model of how to connect up different scenes. And we need to think about the eclecticism of the mainstream as a different model of taste and of investment. Instead of the ironic cynicism that might motivate this eclecticism and tolerance, maybe we can find a reinterpretation along the line, not of "I'm investing in everything because nothing really matters," but rather "I'm investing in everything because everything matters." I think there are possibilities here that we have not begun to explore yet.

[1] Reprinted in Lawrence Grossberg, *Dancing in Spite of Myself: Essays on Popular Culture*. Durham/London: Duke University Press 1997.

[2] An elaboration on the issues touched upon here can be found in Lawrence Grossberg, "Same As It Ever Was? Rock Culture. Same As It Ever Was! Rock Theory," in Karen Kelly, Evelyn McDonnell (eds.), *Stars Don't Stand Still in the Sky: Music and Myth*. New York: New York University Press 1999.

[3] On this connection see Lawrence Grossberg, "Cultural Studies in/and New Worlds" (1993), in Lawrence Grossberg, *Bringing It All Back Home: Essays on Cultural Studies*. Durham & London: Duke University Press 1997; and Lawrence Grossberg, "Speculations and Articulations of Globalization," in *Polygraph* 11 (1999).

[4] See Lawrence Grossberg, *Caught in the Crossfire: Kids, Politics and America's Future*. Boulder, Colorado: Paradigm Publishers 2005.

# *There Is No Global Culture!* Conversation with Meaghan Morris

Interview conducted in August 1999.

The alleged emergence of an increasingly uniform global culture that levels all in its path is one of the platitudes of present-day theory. But whether in old imperial contexts or more recent postcolonial ones, the interactions between different cultural practices and temporalities are too confused to allow a picture of increasing homogenization to be construed. In view of this debate, the Australian Cultural Studies theorist Meaghan Morris proposes a primacy of historically specific situational spaces, a re-evaluation of the current rhetoric of mobility, and the politicization of the deregulated "cultural petite-bourgeoisie."

*Too Soon Too Late*—taken from the title of a film by Jean-Marie Straub and Danièle Huillet (*Trop tôt, trop tard*, 1980/81)—is the name of Meaghan Morris's study on issues of historicity in popular culture.* "Too Soon Too Late" does not apply solely to the unadapted anachronism of many forms of resistance (cultural, migratory, feminist), but also the divergent temporalities that non-Western, non-European and non-hegemonic positions have introduced into the apparently linear flow of a "Western" modernity. Morris takes this as her point of departure for pinning down very specific moments of colonialism within the present rhetoric of displacement and mobility—always with a focus on the political context most familiar to her, that of Oceania. To explain why this approach inevitably returns to the "popular" arenas of Australian beaches, motels or shopping centers, Morris cites the postcolonially informed historicity of these seemingly so interchangeable, "global" sites. But what also become visible are the contours of a Cultural Studies approach that tries to understand cultural change and minorized themes on the basis of a new "industrial way of thinking."

* Meaghan Morris, *Too Soon Too Late: History in Popular Culture*, Bloomington, Indianapolis: Indiana University Press 1998.


Publications by Meaghan Morris:

- *Michel Foucault: Power, Truth, Strategy*. Sydney: Feral Publications 1978 (ed. together with Paul Patton).
- *The Pirate's Fiancée: Feminism, Reading, Postmodernism*. London: Routledge 1988.
- *Australian Cultural Studies: A Reader*. Chicago: University of Illinois Press 1993 (ed. together with John Frow).
- *Too Soon Too Late: History in Popular Culture*. Bloomington, Indianapolis: Indiana University Press 1998.
- *'Race' Panic and the Memory of Migration*. Hong Kong: Hong Kong University Press 2002 (ed. together with Brett de Bary).
- *New Keywords: A Revised Vocabulary of Culture and Society.* Oxford: Blackwell Publishing 2005 (ed. together with Tony Bennett and Lawrence Grossberg).
- *Hong Kong Connections: Transnational Imagination in Action Cinema.* Durham NC and Hong Kong: Duke University Press and Hong Kong University Press 2006 (ed. together with Siu-leung Li and Stephen Ching-kiu Chan).
- *Identity Anecdotes: Translation and Media Culture*. London: Sage Publications 2006.

CH *A central question confronting contemporary Cultural Studies—in its various forms, genealogies and methods—is the problem of history; not only in the sense of its own, often complex and overlaid historicity but also with respect to its "objects," often hailed as the ephemeral, "here and now" products of popular culture. Since you put a strong theoretical emphasis on the notion of history within Cultural Studies—formulated both in terms of desire as well as (theoretical) need—let me ask you what motivates this emphasis in the first place. What relevant dimensions does "history" add to the conduits and practices of everyday life?*

MM Let me make a few comments about the discipline of Cultural Studies before I situate my emphases within it. First, it's important to remember that Cultural Studies is not only the study of popular culture, let alone of contemporary popular culture. "Cultural Studies" can be concerned with sexuality in ancient Rome, with the history of samba in Brazil, or the uses of classical musics in Indian cinema; with the role played by governmental elites in shaping media regimes (a particular interest of mine); with the "birth of the museum," the art gallery, the literary canon, as well as their contemporary uses; with the emergence and effects of the notion of a "national language," and so on. Cultural Studies is not defined by a particular set of topics, but by its analytical interest in the relations between cultural practices on the one hand, and social and economic powers on the other. This means that Cultural Studies is vitally concerned with institutions, and institutions do not live for the "here and now." They have a deep, deep ballast of precedent and custom, and a powerful inertia which acts as a memory.

Second, "contemporary popular culture" itself is not necessarily ephemeral, except perhaps in the trivial sense that its performative aspects may have the fleeting quality of all temporal arts; but the sophistication of our recording, storage and distributional technologies today makes even that assumption dubious. Of course, when people call media culture ephemeral, they usually mean that its products will hold no interest for future generations or even for ourselves next week. That is less and less useful an assumption these days: leaving aside the question of how media genres extensively rework folkloric forms, just look at what cable TV has done to bring old films and TV shows back into currency, or at the destruction of the "hit parade" formation of popular music taste by the proliferation of new and old musics easily available on CD; look at the collapse of the idea of "fashion" as a single set of norms revised by decree each season. Technology and commerce today are promoting restoration, conservation, commemoration, reinterpretation and revision as organizing principles of popular media culture—selectively so, no doubt, but on a massive scale. The terminal and the telephone combined will soon make available a whole archive of popular culture for people to access, and that archive will include popular cultural texts about popular cultural history.

One effect of all this is to make it much more obvious that durability and ephemerality are not intrinsic properties of particular objects and forms of culture—as the "Mozart is durable, Madonna is ephemeral" approach assumes—but the outcome of particular ways of valuing objects and forms. Those ways of valuing are also historical; the idea that media products are ephemeral has itself turned out to be ephemeral, or (to be serious) transitory. Cultural Studies as I understand it, is interested in this too; it can study ephemera, but it can also study the history of "ephemerality" as a modern (and modernist) idea. And it can study the "arts of memory" that people practice in and through their use of the media, and in their ways of participating in popular culture generally. "Culture" in Cultural Studies is always understood as a field of practices, i.e. what people do—and not as a set of objects or texts.

Third, popular culture is not the same thing as everyday life. There is more to everyday life than "culture," popular or unpopular. And just as there are elite forms of everyday life, so there are sacral, momentous or "rare" forms and occasions in popular culture. Cultural Studies is interested in the relations between the elite and the popular, the popular and the everyday, the everyday and the extraordinary. Cultural Studies is also interested in the relations between culture and not-culture, and those relations are profoundly shaped in time as well as by place.

In short: "History" is already inside the conduits and practices of everyday life. It is not something we need to "add" to it. It is always there in institutions, and as a pervasive dimension of experience. History is also produced in everyday life; Cultural Studies rejoins social history on this point. My own work draws attention to this, asking—how do we think about it? How do we talk about the relations between "history" as academics practice it now, and the popular histories and historiographies we encounter every day? Interdisciplinary debate in English-language Cultural Studies has been too preoccupied, in my view, with a scholastic quarrel between "literature" and sociology, aesthetics and the social sciences. In my part of the world, at least, thinking about history in Cultural Studies is a much more pressing need, because Asian and Pacific societies generally are undergoing a period of immense upheaval in which popular conflicts about the value of the past for the present and future are becoming very intense.

## Historically Contingent Contexts

*Your version of Cultural Studies is not only focused on specific historical dimensions and layers of its objects of study, but also concerned with a very precise notion of context. Instead of plunging into the big, global debates often dominant in Cultural Studies, your project is more characterized by a call to clearly define "a context that makes these questions matter." Consequently, you are more engaged with concrete sites and examples of Australian everyday life (and history) than with some free-floating products of an international pop culture. Does this preference of a clearly demarcated geographical or local context parallel the need and desire for historical "deep-structures"? And are such contexts theoretically still sustainable as soon as global processes of media and commodity circulation enter the picture?*

Well, I'd say that I'm more engaged with concrete sites and examples of everyday life in Australia than with the globally circulating products of an international "theory" culture! Let me explain. I don't believe that pop-cultural products (or, for that matter, academic products) ever really do "float free." Products circulate more or less widely (and we can write a political economy of their production and circulation), but that's not the same thing. No matter how widely they circulate, cultural goods are used and consumed by people somewhere; they are taken up in concrete contexts of practice which give them variable meanings and values, and which are always constraining in some way. That context doesn't have to be a nation-state or a region or a city or any sort of physical locale; it can be a transnational profession, or a social movement, or a cult, or an Internet chat-room. Individuals inhabit a diversity of contexts, even "floating" a little between them (some more freely than others), but they do so in more or less limited ways. A particular context can dominate our lives, or it can take up ten minutes a day. So the demarcation of a context in my sense need not involve the fixing of clear geographical borders at all, any more than historical structures need to be thought of as "deep." (They don't.) A context is simply an actual or virtual situation-space of some kind which is shaped not only by social and economic forces but by that shared sense of "what matters"—which, by the way, need not be a lasting or durable sense in order to be consequential.

For that reason I would say yes, understanding a context requires understanding its history, and asking what history means for those involved in the context—which may be "nothing much," in some instances, though not in those

I discuss in my book. But I would say "no" if you are asking me whether I equate history with time with depth, in parallel to an equation of geography with space with "surfaces"; and I would emphatically say "no" if you are asking me whether I think that geographical borders contain and demarcate distinct historical spaces. Not at all. Contexts are relationally defined, and far from making contextual or pragmatic thought unsustainable, global processes are making it indispensable. Contexts are the material support of globalization. To put it another way: there are almost-global cultural industries (of which the English-language academy is rapidly becoming one), and almost-globally available cultural products (Hollywood action movies, for example). But there is no such thing as "global culture," except in the professional imaginary of cultural theorists who write about other theorists without doing empirical research; there are only concrete contexts in which global products are taken up in particular ways. Tony Mitchell's work on the "glocalization" [sic] of rap music makes this very clear.[1] African-American varieties of rap seem to be "global" in a context-erasing way only if you pay no serious attention to Italian varieties of rap, Sa'amoan rap, Maori rap, white boy rap, Canberra rap, indeed, to African re-appropriations of rap … and to the differences as well as the connections between them.

*To follow up on the last question: your project of historical cultural analysis is clearly concerned with the specificity of Australia, in particular, its "Aboriginal past," the British invasion of 1788, its long colonial history, the struggles for decolonization, etc. Do you think it is possible to consider contemporary Australia as an instance of the "postcolonial" and if yes, how could this warrant the assumption that there is a specific Australian context (of culture, postcoloniality, etc.) different from the rest of the postcolonial world?*

Australia can be thought of as "postcolonial" in at least two ways. One is idealistic if not utopian; postcolonialism is the goal toward which we strive, or a becoming that directs contemporary struggles. The other is practical and trivial: at a certain point, you have to declare that a major phase of colonialism has more or less ended (which does not relieve you of the task of understanding new modes of imperialism, and their parasitic relation to the power relations and structures of feeling established by the old modes of imperialism). For some Australians, Australia became "postcolonial" with the passing of the Native Title Act (recognizing the claims of the Aboriginal inhabitants) in 1992–1993. I tend to agree. For others, becoming a republic is the vital step, and that might occur in 2000 or in ten or twenty years' time.

Either way, I wouldn't say that "that there is a specific Australian context different from the rest of the postcolonial world"—because the "rest" of the postcolonial world is not all the same! All postcolonial contexts have their specificity; there is nothing remarkable at that level about any one of them, and to describe that specificity does not entail proclaiming it unique. Indeed, specificity is often best grasped through multiple comparisons and contrasts. One obvious difference organizing "the postcolonial world" is that between former colonies of settlement, where the imperial immigrants stayed on to swamp the native people—Australia, the United States, Canada, Taiwan, for example—and colonies of "occupation," such as India, New Guinea, Algeria, East Timor (the latter group being the one in which postcolonialism is most commonly achieved by nationalizing wars of liberation, the former being more inclined and able—for obvious reasons—to opt for legalistic resolutions of conflict). Obviously, the South African case then stands out as having peculiar features. Less obviously, connections emerge between communities of "settlers" who stay on in former colonies of occupation, or who find themselves living in reconfigured political geographies: think of Northern Ireland, Palestine, Kosovo or, less dramatically, areas of present-day China and Indonesia.

Other kinds of historical mapping are possible. Donald Denoon's book on *Settler Capitalism*[2] compares the experiences of Australia, Canada and New Zealand with Argentina, Paraguay and Uruguay—not in terms of the ethnicity of the imperialists, but in terms of how capitalism developed there depending on whether the invaders encountered hunter-gatherer or "peasant" forms of organization among the indigenous people. And there are "black settler" societies—Liberia, for example. Without going any further, my point is simply that the "rest of the postcolonial world" adds up, one way or another, to "most of the world" these days, and to bring out the complexity of one small part of it is to make a contribution to the much larger task of thinking "history" globally—and not a refusal of that task.

*Judging from* Too Soon Too Late, *your main sites of theoretical interest are places like motels, shopping centers, urban towers, beaches and tourist sights in general. What exactly motivates these choices over—as so frequently practiced in Cultural Studies—the theorization of television series, soap operas, ads, pop songs, etc., in short, all the "traditional" venues of supposedly everyday life empowerment? Does this maybe have to do with wanting to visit "real" places (thought of, of course, as complex fields of antagonistic struggle) as opposed to all the "hyper-real" media images one has been through?*

No, I don't believe in the "hyper-real," and so I don't believe that there is a special sacred or rudimentary zone of the "real" that we have to trace or recover. Everything that exists is real, including the virtual. So media images form just as much a part of my life as the weather in Australia and the air-conditioning in America or the fresh wind in the bush and the stale air in shopping malls. I am primarily a film and television critic, and my current project is about trans-nationally produced martial arts films that are issued on video and the popular historiography that grows up around them. Of course, in a way this is very easy after having dealt with malls, motels and beaches for ten years. Our ability to speak about conventional aesthetic forms, objects and practices—about "texts" (for lack of a more suitable word)—is more highly developed than our ability to use important sites to analyze the "culturalization"—a term I prefer to "aestheticization"—of everyday life in detail and with the necessary differentiation. That is what I tried to do in *Too Soon Too Late*.

## Cultural Change

*One of the main aspects of historical discourse—or the historical dimension within Cultural Studies—is the notion of "cultural change" (be it in the sense of progress or decline). You are less concerned with Big Theory as propelling "change" or "progress" than with the multiplicity of "struggles over the meaning and value of history in the present," which might include different temporalities, liberating potentials, etc. To what extent is this latter notion of "change" informed by minoritarian issues and—if these issues consist in different antagonistic projects—does that not preclude a closure of the term "cultural change" altogether?*

This is a big question, and I've touched on some aspects of my response already. I'd just want to add, first, that I don't see "minoritarian issues" as necessarily involving antagonistic differences; and, second, that if and when they do involve antagonistic difference, they do not necessarily thereby differ from "majoritarian" struggles! I am not a particularist, I should make that clear. On the contrary, I agree with Naoki Sakai's argument in *Translation and Subjectivity*[3] that the relationship between "universalism" and "particularism" is one of profound complicity; they need each other and feed off each other, often at a terrible cost in human suffering. However, one does not need to espouse particularism in order to observe that the definition of what counts as "majoritarian" issues has hitherto been the privilege of special minorities—most often, as the stereotype goes, the privilege of European white men. What can possibly be "minoritarian" about women's issues? About race and racism, or the issues that matter to the immigrants who enable the so-called "host" society to survive and sometimes to thrive? The fact is that we have inherited the model of "antagonistic difference" from the vocabulary of class struggle, the great battle between (white male) capital and (white male) labor. Projected on to cognate or allied "other" struggles, this suddenly becomes a danger or a threat to solidarity. I think this is nonsense. What is confusing and difficult about thinking "change" these days is not that minorities-in-general are running around asserting their particularisms, but rather the proliferation of struggles, including antagonisms and alliances, in the name of which people are demanding recognition and telling their stories in public. The struggles themselves are not new, usually. What is new is the relative legitimacy of their claim to matter as much as the so-called "majority" issues do. So I'd argue that our inherited theories and concepts of change, and not "minorities," are at fault here; they are inadequate to our circumstances, and as intellectuals we need to do something about that. To begin to attempt this is one of the aims of my book.

*A special site of your theoretical interest is the Australian tourist industry and its export image of an urban, socially liberal, multiculturalist heaven (Heaven was also the title of one of Tracey Moffatt's recent video works). Picking out one these epithets, multiculturalism, it seems that this idea became especially important in Australia around the Bicentennial (1988) when revisionist accounts of colonialism became sort of mainstream (as you once mentioned). How would you circumscribe the current state of the multiculturalism debate in Australia? What are its different power vectors? And how is it related to the more and more predominant political culture of "corporatism"?*

The current state of the multiculturalism debate in Australia is wretched. It is true that 1988 and the Bicentennial were a high point both politically and with regard to the intellectual and social field. At the time, people generally seemed to accept that "multiculturalism" could be a philosophy of coherence as well as of difference—a method allowing heterogeneous groups of people to live together. A principle of composition, as Deleuze and Guattari call it.

But this phase ended symbolically in 1996 with the landslide victory of the present Liberal-National government. Looking back, it is clear that the social consensus on multiculturalism as something "that really matters" had begun to crumble much earlier. The reasons for this are complicated, but in my view they were primarily of an economic rather than ideological nature—in other words, there is no return to racism or assimilationism as nation-defining *principles* taking place on a popular basis. Surveys—whatever you may think of them—still suggest that there is broad agreement with the practical principle of multiculturalism running right through society. It's just that people have stopped seeing those particular social themes as having priority, and the term "multiculturalism" has lost its ethical appeal. After all, the Labor government was voted out in 1996 because it seemed to be too interested in "secondary" ethical ideals—Aboriginal rights, feminism and multiculturalism—to the detriment of economic issues that were of more import to "ordinary people" *including* migrants, women and Aborigines. The restructuring of the economy that took place in the 1980s and 1990s had terrible consequences for the working population, especially in rural areas. These people believed that "Labor corporatism" had sold them to so-called "interest groups," that is, to the elitist, self-appointed representatives of the interests of migrants, women and Aborigines. And there's an element of truth in this.

At the moment, the situation is strange, not to say desperate, above all because of the passionate nostalgia of the present prime minister, John Howard, for the old, assimilationist "White Australia" of his youth in the 1950s. Some members of his government do not necessarily share this feeling, but it is unfortunately possible to be socially liberal while at the same time advocating a right-wing, radical economic neoliberalism. This is probably the course that the Liberal Party will take as soon as Howard retires.

Interestingly enough, Howard has not managed to erase the topic of multiculturalism completely from the working vocabulary of the Australian political parties. He was even forced to acknowledge it as one of Australia's most important social achievements. Rhetorically speaking, the "interest groups"—whose interests are in fact neither all that specific nor limited to small groups—have probably temporarily won the day. But at the administrative and imaginary level, "white" Australia has made a comeback in a big way. This is to be deplored, but it will hopefully pass. The demographics of Australia today mean that there is really no way back, but then there is no guarantee that another mode of "paranoid nationalism" (as Ghassan Hage calls it) will not prevail in future.

## Mobility and Displacement

*An important point you make about the history of colonialism—and its Australian "instantiation"—is that the old European model of voyage/mobility versus home/domus becomes doubtful within this specific formation. To quote from one of your essays: "Colonization is precisely a mode of movement, practiced as an occupation of other people's homelands as well as a destruction of their families and homes, that transgresses limits and borders. In and after colonialism, a European voyage/domus distinction loses its oppositional structure."[4] Do you consider this point still relevant in today's rhetoric of mobility and displacement? And, on a more general level, how would you inscribe the relevance of "sense of place and belonging" in current everyday practices that are more and more characterized by forced as well as voluntary mobility?*

Well, this critique of the domus/voyage opposition of course draws on today's rhetoric of mobility and displacement. The latter often takes as its premise a past in which, for most people, stable residency in one place allegedly predominated. But this phenomenon was actually very limited in its distribution—namely, to Europeans who seldom traveled, to exaggerate a point. From their point of view, increasing mobility and mass displacement seem newer and "more catastrophic" than they really are. This can be felt quite clearly in the writings of French authors like Paul Virilio and Jean Baudrillard: Their frightening present-day and future scenarios are based on the narrative of a "human" past in which an extremely stay-at-home peasant gets on a train for the very first time and sees his whole world or way of existence being destroyed. No doubt this was an extremely traumatic experience—or the allegorical version of it is. But at the time when some European peasants where having their very first train-ride, my Irish ancestors were being taught from birth that they would one day inevitably have to emigrate from their ravaged country ("raised to emigrate" as the expression goes). What kind of an experience of "home" do you have when you know from your first conscious moment that you will get on a ship at sixteen, travel ten thousand miles to an unknown country and never see your birthplace or your own mother ever again? What is a "homeland" if displacement is programmed into the experience of "home" from the start? One thing is certain: you can experience a sense of belonging in this way even while you are in transition.

A central problem, then, is how "nation" and historiography should be understood. Even a theorist of nationalism like Ernest Gellner relegates immigrant nations like the USA or huge patched-together nations like India to a footnote. His explanation assumes the superiority and "naturalness" of the Western European model. I am interested in the question of what happens when we make the constitutive migrant experiences of nation-building the central focus; what happens when—for the sake of argument—we relegate the Western European denial of migration as the basis of nationality and citizenship to a footnote? It immediately becomes apparent that today's rhetoric of mobility and displacement sustains more continuity and more complex connections with the old, traditional rhetoric. Once we understand this, we can understand the specificity of the present day much more realistically. And then we gain new insight into the phenomena of immobilization and forced mobility. The latter is even perhaps a defining characteristic of our time; certainly it is appearing on a widening scale. But the forced mobility of some is accompanied by the increasing enclosure of large zones of the population in industrial countries—like the "red-lining" of communities and areas in American cities that are hopelessly in debt and that no bank in the world will give credit to; the immobilization of rural workers and industrial workers who are unable to sell their skills to the new economy, in cities that are slowly dying; but also the "superfluous people" in developing countries. Just think of the huge refugee camps that are full of the victims of economic and political violence, or of natives who—as in Taiwan, Bali, or parts of Australia—are shut into tourism-infested reserves as a result of cultural violence. In this regard I am a "traditionalist": these multicultural histories are still always histories of capital and labor, and perhaps this continuity can be more easily observed today in those countries that were shaped by colonialism from the start.

*Last question, about the social positioning of cultural theorists and critics, or maybe about the self-positioning of Cultural Studies theorists: in today's neoliberally deregulated societies and economies, it seems that cultural workers—be it academics, critics, artist or other "aesthetic technicians"—have fewer and fewer chances* not *to fall into the new emerging class that Bourdieu and other have termed "the new cultural petite-bourgeoisie." Would you agree with this diagnosis? Do you think this is necessarily a deplorable development and if yes, what could be emerging, tactical ways out of this "classification"?*

I agree with this diagnosis, but I think it is only deplorable if we deal with it clumsily or act in a pathetic manner from our status as "the new cultural petite-bourgeoisie." In future, a new politics of cultural workers is sure to develop, that much is clear. But the form these politics will take can at present barely be described or imagined. We are only at the very start of a new phase in the development of capitalism—which is not necessarily a "late" capitalism, but simply unfamiliar in many regards. We are so to speak in the position of Luddites who try to smash up the new machines and fail miserably, but who also shape the space of future politics in the process. So while I do not share Bourdieu's caustic attitude to "media intellectuals," I appreciate the verve of his critical attacks.

But they still seem very European to me; in Australia, as in the USA, the basis of sociality is irreducibly "mediatized," and there is no "outside"—and certainly not at the universities—from which intellectuals could speak. That is why I think accepting our "classification," rather than rejecting it, is the right first step toward a more lively political presence.
The second step would be to think "industrially." Under the present conditions, it has become very hard for the "cultural petite-bourgeoisie" to survive, especially in countries where the apparatus of the welfare state has been demolished, as has largely been the case in Australia, for example. The penalty for economic failure today is so huge that appealing to people's ethos, sense of justice, altruism or social conscience has become almost useless. Political criticism of the old school has become—at the most—an entertainment program or a religious ritual. We have to concentrate much more practically and constructively on how we can organize ourselves "industrially" in the post-welfare-state world. After all, the ethos of criticism needs a huge amount of financial assistance from the state to be able to survive. In European countries, where people have decided to live with high rates of unemployment and to guarantee a certain degree of welfare, this financial assistance has largely been maintained—it ensures the survival of the Bourdieus of our time, which is a good thing. But in the rest of the world, it has gone for good or was never there in the first place. So we have to consider how we deal practically with the consequences, and this is an intellectual challenge of huge dimensions. It seems to me more appropriate to rebel than to become discouraged, or to be content with just deploring this development.

[1] Tony Mitchell, *Popular Music and Local Identity: Rock, Pop and Rap in Europe and Oceania*. Leicester: Leicester University Press 1996.

[2] Donald Denoon, *Settler Capitalism: The Dynamics of Dependent Development in the Southern Hemisphere*. Oxford, New York: Clarendon 1983.

[3] Naoki Sakai, *Translation and Subjectivity: On Japan and Cultural Nationalism*. Minneapolis, London: University of Minnesota Press 1997.

[4] Meaghan Morris , "At Henry Parkes Motel," in *Too Soon Too Late*, p. 62 f.

CHAPTER II

# On Postcolonialism

# *Europe Doesn't Know Its History*
# Conversation with Paul Gilroy

Interview conducted in April 2000.

What does it mean to be a European? Does it still signify—despite all the inner-European fissures—having a culturally dominant, majoritarian, and above all white position? Or shouldn't precisely the historical acts of violence and separation contained in this ascription be brought more to light—especially when the intention is to suggest a comprehensive, supranational unity?

Paul Gilroy started looking at specific European processes of exclusion like these very early on, for example in his book *There Ain't No Black in the Union Jack* (1987),* in which he examined the mutual differentiations between "Blackness" and "Britishness." Or in the influential study on *The Black Atlantic* (1993),** where he highlighted a substantial flip side to European modernity in black transatlantic culture.

In his book *Between Camps*,*** published in 2000, he goes a step further and tries to outline a postcolonial counterprogram to the "race thinking" that is historically so well-established in Europe. Starting from National Socialism, its lasting repertoire of images, its worldwide resonances in separatist movements and finally its inescapable legacy, he proposes a utopian jump: to a slowly emerging end to old, racist divisions; to a Europe that is as open to its barbaric history as to its non-majoritarian margins.

* Paul Gilroy, *'There Ain't No Black in the Union Jack': The Cultural Politics of Race and Nation*. London: Hutchinson 1987.

** Paul Gilroy, *The Black Atlantic: Modernity and Double Consciousness*. Cambridge, Mass.: Harvard University Press 1993.

*** Paul Gilroy, *Between Camps. Nations, Cultures and the Allure of Race*. London: Allen Lane, The Penguin Press 2000. Interestingly, the book was published under a different title in the United States (*Against Race: Imagining Political Culture Beyond the Color Line*. Cambridge, Mass.: Harvard University Press 2000).

Other publications by Paul Gilroy:

- *The Empire Strikes Black: Race and Racism in 1970s Britain*. London: Hutchinson 1982 (ed. together with Hazel Carby).
- *Small Acts: Thoughts on the Politics of Black Cultures*. London/New York: Serpent's Tail 1993.
- *After Empire: Melancholia or Convivial Culture*. London: Routledge 2004.

CH Between Camps *sets out to argue from what you diagnose as the "current crisis of race-thinking," or raciology, to the (hoped-for) conclusion that there is a new, planetary humanism, a "rootless cosmopolitanism," emerging. As regards the premise of the book—the crisis of raciology—let me first ask you where exactly, in which areas and instances, you would locate the symptoms of this crisis, both culturally and politically, as well as scientifically?*

PG You're right, my new book speaks about a crisis of raciology defined as the lore that brings the virtual realities of "race" to life. It engages Frantz Fanon's project of a new humanism, but that is not so much about celebrating the emergence of a "rootless cosmopolitanism" (a phrase that is interesting only insomuch as it was a term of abuse employed by the Nazis). I am interested in cosmopolitanism, but in its rooted, planetary varieties. The crisis of raciology lies firstly in the impact of the biotech revolution.

It's by no means clear that the old definitions of "race" will be able to survive that new shift unmodified. Secondly, the America-centered definitions of blackness as abjection are retreating because blacks in the US are the producers of some of the most attractive "software" in the new global market. I'm not saying, of course, that this development solves the problem of racism, but rather that we need to take account of the new patterns it creates. Thirdly, there are now hordes of dissenting young people, particularly in the overdeveloped world, for whom the idea of race has no meaning and for whom the hybridization of culture is a routine and entirely unexceptional event. Fourthly, in the lives of postcolonial cities across the world, new ways of living and relating to one another have been devised that make the race hierarchies of the old colonial period untenable. Fifthly, there are emergent ecological and anti-corporate movements that speak to the contradictions of globalization in ways that are significant, as well as a trans-local culture of human rights that relegates race to the realm of "narcissism of minor differences." These things combine with deep changes in the significance of nation-states, national governments and cultures to change the terms in which we should approach the politics of "race" and racism. None of these developments guarantees a progressive outcome. But taken together, they contribute to a new climate in which we can cultivate a new relation with ourselves and return to the problem of species in a new spirit. I have tried to say as well that anti-racism needs a new moral core, a moral transfusion. That's why my book has a utopian flavor. We're so used to saying what we're against that we don't say what we favor very clearly. That has to change as well.

*As for your diagnosis of a "crisis of race-thinking": judging intuitively, isn't there something of the opposite trend taking place at the moment, something like the re-emergence and proliferation of "race" in all different kinds of cultural and political settings? For the latter, one only has to look at the controversial government formation in Austria in 2000, which included an openly racist party that had won almost 30 percent of the votes, or at the still unbroken white supremacist stance that prevails all over Europe (for example, according to a EU survey in 2000, 48 percent of the French consider themselves to be "quite" or "very" racist). Not to mention countless instances of ethnic violence erupting all over the globe. Doesn't "race"—even if it is sometimes openly discarded—re-appear almost everywhere, even in everyday discourse, at least under the rubric of unbridgeable cultural difference?*

You are right to point to the grim evidence from all over the world that "race" and racism are resurgent. I can't deny that there are racisms everywhere, that they are vicious and that ultra-nationalisms of various kinds are a real obstacle to democracy and justice. My book says that we should recognize these things and approach them via a systematically comparative and transnational method. That they need to be seen in the enduring shadow of the war against fascism, but also that the history of that period has to be re-conceptualized and re-written so that being European can no longer mean being white.

The fact that racism and nationalism are ubiquitous and violent doesn't mean that race thinking is historically resurgent. They could be happening because the historic codes of race thinking are breaking down. We could read these events as symptoms of the breakdown, the decay of race thinking prompted by the fact that absolute identity cannot bear the weight that political interests are placing upon it. Globalization makes people anxious. They resolve their ontological and ethnic anxieties into a politics of identity and their anxieties over identity into a politics of ethnicity and nationality. We need to know why those are the attractive and habitable options. We need to be able to show them that nationalisms are not the answer to their anxieties. We need to re-narrate national identities on different scales and address the integrity of the idea of Europe so that its colonial patterns become visible again. Europeans don't know their own history. That's why my book focuses momentarily on the role of black soldiers (colonial and American) in the war against Hitlerism and on the connections between that political morality and the moral claims articulated by the decolonizing movements later on during the cold war.

*Your argument suggests that we are witnessing (or are close to) the end of the color line that was so disastrous in history. Now just as an episode—in protests against the World Bank and the IMF that happened in Washington in April 2000, there seemed to be mostly white protesters on the one side, and mostly black policemen on the other. How would you assess such—again, dividing—developments with respect to the approach you choose?*

It's interesting to me that of all the possible stories you might want to tell about the protests against the World Bank and the IMF in Washington, you are drawn to the confrontation between white protesters on the one side, and mostly black policemen on the other. That is certainly an American story: the story of America's apartheid. It suggests that the meaning of those protests is best told in those "local" terms. For me, there are lots of other things to say about that confrontation in Washington. It raises issues of planetary consciousness, of responsibility and accountability, trans-local solidarity and political agency on a global basis against an unjust and unsustainable system that creates American prosperity at the price of condemning most people on this planet to servitude and starvation. To me, the police in that confrontation with the demonstrators are just American police put there to do a specific violent job by their government. I think it's a big mistake to choose to bring the American story of race difference alive in the way that demonstration is understood. To be drawn in that direction would mean a defeat for the overall politics of the event. Of course, the people who made that into a big issue in the US media were very much alive to the "divide and rule" dynamics involved. But let's be clear about one thing: because people are black, that doesn't make them automatically radical, anti-capitalist or anything like that. Those cops are in many, many ways just regular American guys doing their jobs.

## Camp Mentality

*Coming back to the notion of national self-assurance, I would briefly like to talk about what you outline as the "camp mentality" of the modern nation-state and modern governmentality. Isn't this hidden trope of modernity on the rise again everywhere, especially as regards the alleged erosion of nation-state borders, be it by global economic deterritorialization, or by the purposeful and guided construction of hyper-national units like the EU? It almost seems as if for a lot of people, this mentality appears as a last residue or anchor against economic or globalizing processes of de-centering.*

I've used the trope of the camp and the idea of the "camp mentality" to accomplish a certain conceptual and rhetorical task. I've used it to underline the relations, the affinities between nationalisms and fascism on the one hand, and colonial history and European history on the other. I don't know if it's a hidden trope of modernity. I wanted to consider race and nation in relation to 1) the life of sovereign territories, and 2) the geo-political codes of national statecraft and national identity, particularly in authoritarian regimes. There are at least two different ideas of space at work here. One that derives from Haushofer, Kjellén and co., the path that leads to Carl Schmitt's theories of geo-piety and geo-politics; and the other that derives from the English tradition of Hobbes and Locke and produces the colony as a nomos of a distinctive type. I'm sure you're right when you point out that these ways of belonging, of linking place and being are increasingly attractive as an antidote to the anxieties of globalization.

*As regards the "camps," which of course refer not only to a mode of modern political thought, but also to the actual barbarisms of the Nazi camps as well as to colonial contexts, I wanted to follow up with a brief question: as the title of the British edition of your book (not the American one) suggests, you favor and argue for a position "between camps" (I will come back later to what that exactly means). But for now, I wanted to ask if it wouldn't be favorable to argue for doing away with camp discourse, with camps in all their variable forms, altogether? Or what would be the advantage of arguing for a position "in-between camps," thereby possibly still acknowledging the legitimacy of such camps?*

The title of my book really is *Between Camps*. The US publishers changed it without my permission. I take that phrase to be our political and historical address. That's where we live and where we need to be in order to find a moral and political orientation in these difficult times. Of course, I have tried to give additional value to the experience, the predicament of being in-between, to present it as being SOMEWHERE, a place from which critical observations and interventions can be made. It gains in power for me when that idea is linked directly to the concept of diaspora and the explicitly anti-national orientation that diaspora sensibilities have regularly engaged. This is not to romanticize displacement, but to say that it can bring insights as well as deprivation and suffering.

*With respect to current modes of cultural or political belonging, your argument is very much inclined toward a new set of always provisional, relational and negotiated identities without any fixed "roots." Now of course, this model was laid out by you in the diasporic identity formation of the Black Atlantic*[1]*—a very influential approach that is based on notions of mixture, syncretism and constant re-adaption/re-negotiation. Would you consider this form of identity (or identity formation process) as valid or available for ALL dislocated people, regardless of their social, educational, etc. status? In other words, is it really "available" on a thoroughly popular level, or should it maybe, more realistically, be confined to a sort of cultural elite or avant-garde?*

No, I'm really against the idea that the hybridity option is only available to those people who turn left when they get on board the plane. That's too pessimistic, and often that critique of my position is offered in bad faith. Michael Ignatieff, Jonathan Friedman and the other connoisseurs of difference who are setting themselves up as policemen seem to believe that they're the only ones who are allowed to move around the world freely. The problems start when all those noisy black people arrive and start upsetting the pensioners, who are then seen as legitimate in their dislike of foreigners and strangers. Those critics have never been anti-racists of any sort. They have never recognized the dignity and integrity of approaching justice and democracy through the test that anti-racism supplies to liberal political cultures. Firstly, the debate about hybridity has always been at source, an argument about the experiences of immigrants and their non-immigrant children. It's about saying that the role of the so-called "second-generation immigrant" is an absurdity. The loudest voices against my argument all mystify and conceal that obvious point. Secondly, if you look at the life of the postcolonial world cities, you'll see not only that "culture is ordinary," as Raymond Williams put it, but that hybridity is ordinary too. It's become a routine, banal element in the workings of ordinary life. It's here that utopia becomes not the sign of placeless-ness, but the name of the good-place, the good city. We can bring back Thomas More's original pun.

I know that globalization accentuates the divisions between those who can move and those who are trapped. But even those who cannot move are thinking their identities and experiencing their being in the world via trans-local processes of various types, not least the trans-local media-scape[2] of the infotainment tele-sector.

*Let me now come to your crucial claim that the current developments in biotechnology, like locating the body's essence in the genes, can be considered as a move away from openly racist forms of "epidermalization" or visual regimes of racism that were most prominently at work in the colonial context. Doesn't biotechnology, with its own essentialist and deterministic attitudes toward the body, give rise to an equally dangerous form of body-politics? A body-politics that has close ties to historical forms of eugenics or to a renewed ideology of "biological fitness"? How do you assess the alleged obsolescence of race in that light?*

If the biotech revolution gives rise to a new body-politics it will not be a body-politics in which the idea of race will be comfortably situated. That's not to say that it will be alright. Only that it won't be racist in ways that we can recognize from the past. It might be a good deal worse than the wrongs that were done before in the name of "race." We can be sure that the genetic underclass won't be anything like the racial types of old.

## Black Popular Culture

*This brings me to an important shift that you lay out in your book and that is central to an adequate understanding of the role of race in current popular culture. As regards black popular culture—or the disseminated counterculture of the Black Atlantic—you register an important historical shift from an identity politics (still present in 1970s soul and funk, as in George Clinton's slogan "free your mind and your ass will follow,"[3]) to a sort of "racialized bio-politics" (present in a lot of recent hip-hop, most notably gangsta rap, and in sports). On the one hand, the new body-centered bio-politics does seem to leave old racial or separatist discourses (of a distinct black identity) behind, on the other, it does of course produce a lot of new stereotypes as well. Do you see any chance of this ambivalence's being made politically productive, or is this development doomed altogether?*

I'm not sure that we can bring the moral energy and political critique of the 1970s movement back to life. I see the conflict here between the cultures of privatization and custodial corporeality and a more old-fashioned culture of the public good. There are a few residual elements in hip-hop culture that speak to the continuing resonance of the old political language from that time. I like the idea that there is still a commitment around to claiming the body back from the world of work, wages etc. There are other ways of being free and experiencing one's own power than the ones that corporate multi-culturalism creates. We dance, don't we? The rave culture is strong and compelling because it gives glimpses of a world beyond this one and a system of values that turns away from the specifications of the market. We have to be able to make it as easy to imagine the end of capitalism as it is currently to imagine the end of the world.

*Concerning corporate multiculture—which does a lot to market these images of freaky black bodies or black supermen or sports heroes, and which you sharply distinguish from the political project of multiculturalism—you lay out a surprising sort of cultural genealogy which goes back to the centralization of the image and of visuality in general (or of unifying logos) as favored and pushed by the political project of the Nazis. Throughout your book, you also come up with a lot of revealing intersections between Nazism and black separatist discourses. But does that genealogy—in the form of a particular "fascist glamour"—really reach out so far as to determine the current dominance of visuality within mass culture?*

Concerning corporate multiculture, we have to confront the legacies of Leni Riefenstahl that apply to the postmodern cultures of health and fitness. Those legacies exist both inside and outside of democracy. That moment in 1936 set incredibly durable patterns that still reoccur in the dreamscape of this consumer capitalism. How many sports ads replicate elements of her Olympiad? Why should these particular symbols and patterns of coding the body be so powerful? How do they help us to understand where the line might be drawn between fascist modernity and supposedly more healthy varieties? Do you know Robert Proctor's fantastic book *The Nazi War On Cancer*[4]? It seems to me that he's making the same point on very different ground, but asking similar questions about their modernity and ours.

*As I said, it is very revealing and striking how you elaborate a lot of parallels between Nazism and its violent quest for purity and national rebuilding, and fraternalist, masculinist purity-seekers on the "black" side of the old racial color-line, so to speak. Would you really go so far as to say that there is sort of universal fascist pattern in all these different historical movements or instances? Or could one maybe regard this parallel or relatedness itself as a form of "global" hybridization or syncretism (such as Marcus Garvey talking about "African Lebensraum"), thereby supporting your argument about constant cultural intermixture, even on a level where one would expect it the least?*

Black people are not permanently confined in a different moral universe from other people on this planet. To have been a victim of racism doesn't guarantee that you'll always be an anti-racist, never mind a democrat. We hunger for innocent identities, but everybody can do the wrong thing. The fraternal alliance of purity-seekers certainly does show that there is what Primo Levi called "a silent Nazi diaspora" spreading around the world. The situation becomes even more complicated when we have to recognize that there are mimics as well as fascists and neofascists around. They aren't all the same, but they are connected to each other.

*In outlining a positive and promising version of multiculturalism, you draw heavily on the model of the Black Atlantic counterculture that has been around at least since the late eighteenth century (with figures like Phillis Wheatley or Olaudah Equiano). This counterculture gained its most significant momentum in the emergence of a musical movement, starting, amongst other things, with ethnically mixed American military bands that came to Europe in the aftermath of World War I. Why was it particularly music that became such an important mainstay of this alternative modernity and countercultural diasporic movement—more than, say, anything in the visual arts? And how is that musical movement itself transformed by the current phase of multiculture's global marketing?*

The American military bands that came to Europe in the aftermath of the First World War were not ethnically mixed. They were black bands of men who had been soldiers fighting the Kaiser often in the French Army, not the American one. That story interested me not just because it gave me a new insight into Adorno's view of jazz as militaristic and fascistic music, but because it seemed to point to the special things that black music has done for, to and with European modernism. The music becomes important because, as an essentially non-representational form, it is hard to discipline and because it repudiates the authority of the purity seekers by being both protean and learnable. Today it can be reduced to the role of a soundtrack for somebody's commercial. That is a reversal of its historic role and translatable, trans-local power.

## Planetary Humanism

*You conclude the book with an outlook on a "planetary humanism" or a "rootless cosmopolitanism" in which—to evoke the words of Frantz Fanon—the "color of skin should have no more significance than the color of eyes (until then, there will be war)." This is a decidedly utopian conception, and I am wondering how that fits in with a lot of scenarios where "skin" (to put it provocatively) or ethnicity should be granted at least a certain affirmative status, one in terms of minority rights, entitlement, rehabilitation for suffered injustice, etc. In other words, should difference not be granted a certain protected status—one that could then be acknowledged in the important on-going processes of cultural translation?*

*Between Camps* is a modest contribution to the making of a new humanism, the newness of which is revealed to reside precisely in the ways that it has been systematically disenchanted by the difficult work of understanding of how "race" damaged the humanisms of the past. That detour through modern histories of suffering must become obligatory. It provides a means to locate ethical and political principles that can guide the work of building more just and equitable social relations. This is not anti-racism of the type that says we must learn to love and value rather than fear human differences. It feels like a new project because it is prepared to break with the notion that racial differences are a self-evident fact of political life. It refuses the idea that this order of difference is somehow necessary to the very stability of our conflicted world. Instead it suggests that the reification of race can be challenged and that the narcissism of minor differences is an especially destructive force in the fields of "race" and ethnicity. It seeks to turn the tables on purity-seekers whoever they may be, to force them to account for their phobia about otherness and hostility in the face of the clanging, self-evident sameness of humankind. It wants the words "the human race" to recover the incendiary, revolutionary force that they had in earlier phases of modern life. If by saying that racialized differences should be granted a special status you mean that they should be guaranteed rights of recognition under the Hegelian formulae of hospitable liberalism, then I'm wary of that strategy. Of course in post-slave states or places where there are histories of suffering and genocide close to hand there may be specific obligations placed upon the polity, but I'd prefer these to be rationalized in terms of justice rather than ethnicity. Also, I favor an approach which is less inclined to the dynamics of recognition and more concerned with the justice of discrimination. I think we could frame adequate "anti-racist" statutes in those terms.

*To follow up on that last point, let me sketch a bleak and negative scenario of the present: the purity-seekers of right-wing movements are of course not into any version of the equivalence of different cultural contexts. Difference for them is very much an unbridgeable affair. But what they are primarily into is a suprematist, fully privatized and deregulated economics that takes advantage of any inequalities there are (not just cultural or racial ones). Now, in order to fight their massive racist stance—and in order to really overcome the color line—would it not be crucial to challenge them on a primarily economic level?*

Of course they should be challenged on an economic level. They should be opposed on every level. My point is that their pursuit of purity obeys different logics, rationalities etc. than the formal procedures set by our sense of the rules under which they operate. Raciology, from Chamberlain on down, doesn't have a problem in balancing occult and scientific discourses. These days the workings of spin and PR etc. mean that politicians will say anything they need to say to protect their position or initiative. That too is a legacy of the fascist revolution in communications and information of the iconizing and theatricalizing of the process of politics.

*The strategic universalism you outline has a strong futuristic component. For sketching this kind of post-racial universalism, you invoke quite a lot of Afro-futurist cultural endeavors, ranging from Sun Ra and George Clinton's* Mothership Connection *to Afrika Bambaataa's* Planet Rock *and movies like* Men in Black. *How would you say that these cultural futurisms translate back into the social realm? Or, in other words, how can these techno-scientific fantasies be cast back onto an "experiential" cosmopolitanism—one that is itself articulated with the actual experiences of today's multiple diasporas?*

I guess I'd say we have to become more future-oriented and try to moralize the order we favor. Giving flesh and substance to the utopia that corresponds to this moment of globalization can be a philosophical task. We know now what the economic forms of globalization might contain, we have some idea what its cultural dynamics will consist of. What we need to see are its political forms. What will they be and where will they address the question of racialized differences? I'd say that a detour through the history of raciologies becomes an essential move at this point. Only when we've completed that course will it be safe, for a moment, to move back toward the precious goal of that humanism Fanon wrote about.

[1] Paul Gilroy, *The Black Atlantic: Modernity and Double Consciousness*.
[2] Cf. Arjun Appadurai, *Modernity at Large: Cultural Dimensions of Globalization*. Minneapolis, London: University of Minnesota Press 1996, p. 33 ff.
[3] The title of a record by the band Funkadelic in 1970.
[4] Robert Proctor, *The Nazi War On Cancer.* Princeton: Princeton University Press 1999.

# *Africa in Motion*
# Conversation with Achille Mbembe

Interview conducted in September 2002.

For some time, the postcolonialist researcher Achille Mbembe has been studying forms of political and cultural power on the African continent in the wake of colonialism. His main focus is on the emergence of an "Afro-cosmopolitan" culture, including its associated artistic processes.

In the course of the last decade, the cultural production of individual African countries had come to Western attention as an example of the way "world culture" could reshape itself. Although there is still disparaging talk of a "world province" or periphery, there have now long been approaches, both of an artistic and a theoretical nature, that call into question the one-sidedness of these characterizations. Whereas "Africa" used to have negative connotations within Western discourse, whether as the "Dark Continent," the "Heart of Darkness," or as a self-destructive "hole in world history," recent postcolonial approaches are concerned with a locally informed rewriting of these externally imposed "negations."

Achille Mbembe, who was born in Cameroon and teaches at the University of the Witwatersrand in Johannesburg, has attempted in a series of studies to provide the discourse about "Africa" with a historically adequate and complex foundation. His book, *On the Postcolony*[1], is a determined endeavor to see the balance of power in the sub-Saharan countries—above all, Cameroon, Nigeria, Ghana, Senegal, Ivory Coast, Benin, etc., which have been independent for some 40 years—against the background of the continuing colonial legacy and new international and regional influences. In his work, Mbembe covers themes ranging from the "banality" or "vulgarity of power," demonstrated in the first decades of independence above all in the figure of the postcolonial autocrat and his lavish rituals of state culture, to contemporary and controversial forms of "private indirect government."[2] As a consequence of the latter, state sovereignty, economic interests and power monopolies on the entire continent are tending to slide into a shadowy privatized area that is not answerable to any form of public scrutiny.

Mbembe thus sees both the various grotesque and obscene formations on whose basis the postcolonial regimes functioned at first, and the intensity of partly private, ethnically motivated, and arbitrarily administered violence, which has increased abruptly over the past decade, as being central factors in African governmental systems. This is demonstrated equally by the re-burgeoning of "local" identities that are maintained by paramilitary means, and by the erosion of the state to be seen on all sides. However: "What, in the short run, has every appearance of chaos represents, in the long run, a violent resurgence of struggles over inequality and control of the means of coercion."[3] At first, this gives the impression of being an uninterrupted continuation of the myth of Africa as an endless reservoir of violence and negativity, as a history-less, chaotic "gap in world time." And yet Mbembe's historically circumspect inferences go toward showing how the global, complex interpenetration of autonomy and heteronomy is also producing new and fluid geographies of power on the African continent.

An "Africa in Motion" that liberates itself from the pupation and "zombification" of the colonial era: this is something the progenitor of today's discourses on postcolonialism and liberation, Frantz Fanon, wanted over 40 years ago. Mbembe, who takes up this legacy, has at first supplemented this concept with a new cartography of Africa.[4] Taking this as a basis, his diagnosis is that, in the face of the present situation, not only is the rhetoric of anti-imperialism exhausted, but also the discourse of "self-victimization." It is just as impossible to postulate ONE Africa, based on an ominous ethnic unity, as it is to maintain a collective "victim cult" (something which Mbembe condemns in the strongest terms). The many internal differences, ranging from different lines of tradition to religious surrogate regimes to the numerous, "extra-territorial" war fronts, suggest that the old, central contrast "Africa against the West" has now lost much of its legitimacy. Still, it needs to be seen how "modes of self-writing" can be developed in this situation.[5]

[1] Achille Mbembe, *On the Postcolony*. Berkeley, Los Angeles, London: University of California Press 2001. See also the roundtable reviews on the H-Africa Network, http://www.h-net.org/~africa/

[2] Cf. Achille Mbembe, *On the Postcolony*, p. 66–101.

[3] Ibid., p. 77.

[4] See Achille Mbembe, "At the Edge of the World – Boundaries, Territoriality, and Sovereignty in Africa," in *Public Culture* 12, 1 (2000), p. 259–284 and the visual rendering of this "new geo-political situation in Africa" by Philippe Rekacewicz, "Mapping Concepts," in *Public Culture* 12, 3 (2000), p. 703–706.

[5] See Achille Mbembe, "African Modes of Self-Writing," in *Public Culture* 14, 1 (2002), p. 239–273, as well as the roundtable symposium, "African Modes of Self-Writing Revisited," in *Public Culture* 14, 3 (2002).

CH *In your book* On the Postcolony, *you set out to describe the conditions under which contemporary social reality, or realities, across the African continent came about. What is intriguing at first sight is that you are targeting a single political-historical constellation that spans the whole continent. How important was it, or still is for you, to pay close attention to the manifold local differences—different marks of globalization, so to speak, that imprint themselves in quite different ways in different African territories? What, on the other hand, motivates the quest for a model of one "postcolony"?*

AM In the conclusion of *On the Postcolony*, I explicitly distance myself from this "montage." I argue that the reality with which I have been concerned throughout the book exists only as a set of sequences and connections that extend themselves only to dissolve. It is a reality that is made up of superstitions, narratives and fictions that claim to be true in the very act through which they produce the false, while at the same time giving rise to terror, hilarity and astonishment. Indeed, I define the postcolony as a time-space characterized by proliferation and multiplicity. As a temporal formation, the postcolony is definitely an era of dispersed entanglements, the unity of which is produced out of differences. From a spatial point of view, it is an overlapping of different, intersected and entwined threads in tension with one another. Here, the task of the analyst is to tease out those threads, to locate those intersections and entwinements. This can only be done if, from the start, we take seriously the very compositeness of the postcolony.

Now if, as you suggest, there is a limit to the methodological approach I use in the book, it is certainly that the latter still relies, to a large extent, on social science epistemologies. In spite of substantive attempts (especially in chapter five and six), the rupture with such epistemologies is still not radical enough. I wish I could have made it clearer that what is called Africa is first and foremost a geographical accident. It is this accident that we subsequently invest with a multitude of significations, diverse imaginary contents, or even fantasies, which, by force of repetition, end up becoming authoritative narratives.

As a consequence of the above, what we call "Africa" could well be analyzed as a formation of desires, passions and undifferentiated fantasies. It is a subjective economy that is cultivated, nurtured, disciplined and reproduced. To nurture it, to police it and to reproduce it involves an intensive work of the imagination. But it also entails a tremendous labor of bad faith that the social-science discourse does not know how to deal with.

*What has mostly become known under the heading "postcolonialism" in the West is a discourse vastly concerned with the identity formation and symbolic dwellings of migrant subjects, now living in the Western metropolis. Your take on the "postcolony" seems to substantially differ from that discourse in several aspects, for example insofar as your focus of attention is decidedly directed toward Africa, and you pay particular attention to the material basis of contemporary social realities. How exactly would you describe your departure from the "Western" form of "postcolonialism"?*

There is no doubt that postcolonial theory, under its many guises, has decisively contributed to the "unmasking" of

Western hegemony in the field of the humanities and in other disciplines. It has forced Western discourses on the self and the other, on difference and alterity, or on particularity and universality, to become accountable. In the process, postcolonial theory has revealed the violence of Western epistemologies and the dehumanizing impulses at the heart of their definition of the human. This task is far from over. In fact, it has become all the more urgent, especially in these times of ours when the ultimate expression of imperial sovereignty seems to reside, to a large extent, in the power and the capacity to dictate who may live and who must die.

In such a context, it seems to me that postcolonial theory would gain a lot by reframing its foundational interrogations. When sovereign power has taken control over mortality and has defined life as the very site of the manifestation of absolute power, we need to start asking different questions. One such question is: Under what practical conditions is the right to kill, to allow to live or to expose to death exercised? Who is the subject of this right? What does the implementation of such a right tell us about the entity that is put to death and about the relation of enmity that sets it against its murderer? How can we account for the contemporary ways in which the political, under the guise of war, of resistance or of the fight against terror, makes the murder of the enemy its primary and absolute objective? Such a way of defining the issues raises a number of empirical and philosophical questions postcolonial theory has to address if it is still to be intellectually relevant.

The other challenge to postcolonial theory is what is referred to as "globalization." Whether this process is old or new is somewhat irrelevant. What is clear is that it opens an awareness beyond the postcolonial theory of the 1980s and the 1990s.

*Concerning the prefix "post" in "postcolony," one could wonder (as you do yourself in the book) if history has really moved into a stage past the colonial period. What qualitative differences have occurred on the African continent that would legitimate the use of the term "postcolony" (as opposed to, say, "ex-colony")?*

As far as Africa is concerned, colonialism is over. Apartheid is over too. Africans are now the free masters of their own destiny. This is why from an intellectual and political point of view, there is no turning away from the difficult work of freedom. It is very risky work because it involves a transformative relation with our past as a condition sine qua non of our control over our own future.

Unfortunately, African criticism has been slow to awake to this new reality and its empowering possibilities. The discourse of victimization and resentment is still pervasive. In most African nativist,[1] nationalist or Afro-Marxist discourses, history is still interpreted as an endless process of sorcery. And because history is akin to witchcraft, many feel the need to wear masks and to blame everything on the past. In the process, they forget to account for the self-destruction and self-inflicted injuries that our boundless passions have always incited—and continue to incite.

What this means is that the "post" in "postcolony" does not refer at all to the idea of a regulated transition from one form to another form or duration. We cannot think in terms of a mechanical succession of ages. But in our attempt to create an impression of continuity, we cannot refer to the present and to its actors as simply shadow puppets of something or of somebody else. In my mind, the notion of the "postcolony" refers to a time-scape which is simultaneously in the process of being formed and of being dissolved through a movement that brings both the "being formed" and the "being dissolved" into collision. The term "postcolony" indicates my desire to take very seriously the intrinsic qualities and power of "contemporaneousness" while firmly keeping in mind the fact that the present itself is a concatenation of multiple temporalities. Because of the entanglement of these multiple temporalities, Africa is evolving in multiple and overlapping directions simultaneously.

## Power and Entanglement

*In close relation to the issue of the "post-ness" of contemporary African living situations stands the specific time-model you develop with respect to the age of decolonization. How could this model of "entanglement" —that is, of multiple temporalities overlapping and superseding each other, sometimes inside each other, which is clearly non-linear—warrant the assumption that we have actually moved beyond the framework installed by the colonial regimes?*

To say that colonialism or apartheid is over does not mean to negate history or to erase memory. It simply means to be attentive to those signs of the times which signal the entry into other configurations of human experience, hope and possibilities, or if you wish, other temporalities. As we can clearly infer from everyday life examples, those temporalities almost always carry with them bits and pieces, traces and fragments of the past. These fragments are recycled and imbued with new meanings.

Whether in the cultural, political or symbolic realms, the African present is formed by an assemblage of signs and symbols and artifacts that mean different things in various languages and contexts. These signs, symbols and artifacts are then organized around multiple central tropes that come to function as both images and mirages, parables and allegories. As a result, because it succeeds in weaving onomatopoeic relations between the thing and its double, African cultural history is the perfect archive of resemblance. This is valid for the past and for the present.

*What is particularly striking and original about your approach is the way you theorize power or "commandement" in the "postcolony." Concerned with "the banality of power,"*[2] *you put the Bakhtinian model of the grotesque and the obscene (as possible models of resistance against the oppressor) to a quite distinctive use, in so far as these categories are exactly the modes in which power is exercised (mostly by autocrats) in African postcolonies. What kind of power constellation did, or does, this process exactly engender—for example, you talk of a "mutual zombification" resulting from this?*

The book is not a reflection on power in general, but on that specific formation of will, desire and fantasy that the postcolonial potentate is. This formation of will, fantasy and passions operates predominantly through the mediation of the body and the senses. It is a formation in which power is ubiquitous both in presence and in the realm of the tactile. Its language is that of "jouissance." It appeals not to reason as a category of public life, but to sensations (the eye, the ear, the mouth, the phallus, taste, smell, a range of pleasures and pains of varying intensities). Such a power formation indeed has a historicity and a materiality, as I show in chapters one and two. But more importantly, it is a bundle of energies and brutal fantasies which always end up taking on lives of their own. Because of sheer coercive repetition, these fantasies end up becoming a "habitus" or at least part of the stylistics of everyday life, a prosaics.

More radically, the starkness and the brutality of these fantasies may, on occasion, assume a nightmarish appearance, as reality and fable reflect each other, thereby transforming the very identity of the original and its referents. This is why an analysis à la Foucault or a reading from within the usual categories of political economy are unable to highlight its complexities. In this kind of power formation, reality is each time erased, recreated and duplicated. It is this power of proliferation (and its ability to obliterate the distinctions between truth and falsehood, the visible and the occult) that turns domination and subjection into a magical song, at that point where the originary arbitariness produces terror and hilarity.

*This specific "banality of power" creates a particular closeness between ruler and ruled, a form of "conviviality" or "intimate tyranny" that goes far beyond the binary conceptions of oppressor and oppressed, resulting in powerlessness. In which parts of Africa does this constellation still apply today, and which parts have—in what ways—moved ahead of these excess-driven intimacies of postcolonial domination?*

These power formations are still alive in varying degrees and qualities in those countries where the limits of democratization are the most evident: Cameroon, Togo, Gabon, Kenya, Ivory Coast, Zimbabwe, the Central African Republic, Chad, Burkina-Faso, Liberia or even Nigeria. This said, one can argue that by the end of the 1990s, the political economy of statehood in Africa had dramatically changed. As countries such as South Africa moved away from the most grotesque and ugly forms of violation, other regions of the continent became engulfed in bloody processes of destruction of human bodies and populations (Congo, Angola, Sierra Leone, Sudan, Ethiopia, Eritrea, Rwanda, Burundi). In those instances, the calculus of domination ceased to be embedded in the myriad dispositifs of disciplinary power that had characterized the postcolonial commandement. After all, what was so typical of the commandement was the exchange between obedience and theatricality on one hand, and the redistributive imperative on the other.

Today, in many instances, the commandement has been replaced by a new form of sovereign power: "Necropower."[3] Why necropower? Well, because the ultimate site of deployment of this new form of sovereignty is no longer the body as such, but the dead body of the "civilian." Necropower is wielded both by states and by what, following Deleuze and Guattari, we should call "war machines." War machines are made up of segments of armed men that split up, merge and superimpose each other depending on the circumstances. Polymorphous and diffuse organizations, war machines are characterized by their capacity for metamorphosis. They combine a plurality of functions and operate through capture, looting and predation.

In the context of the multiplication of war machines, technologies of destruction have become more tactile, more anatomical, in a context where the choice today is no longer between obedience and simulation but between life and death. Whether in Sierra Leone or in the Congo, it is easy to note that technologies of destruction are less concerned with inscribing bodies within disciplinary apparatuses as inscribing them, when the time comes, within the order of the maximal economy now represented by the "massacre." We have seen how, during the war in Sierra Leone for example, physical amputation replaced immediate death, and how the cutting off of limbs opened the way to the deployment of techniques of incision, ablation that had bones as their target.

## Private Indirect Government

*Projected transitions to democracy seem to be hunted, across the continent, by the emergence of what you call "private indirect government." Within these new configurations of power, the privatization of violence (as evidenced in the myriad militias and private armies) and of sovereignty goes hand in hand with the "informalization" of large parts of the economy. How did this new form of domination come about and what role did international institutions such as the IMF and the World Bank play in it?*

Democracy as a form of government and as a culture of public life does not have a future in Africa—or for that matter, elsewhere in the world—if it is not rethought precisely from the crucible of "necropower." By "necropower," I have in mind the various ways in which, in our contemporary world, sovereign power imagines itself and is deployed in the interest of maximum destruction of persons and the creation of death-scapes, new and unique forms of social existence in which vast populations are subjected to conditions of life conferring upon them the status of living dead.

Let me hasten to say that this is far from being a typically African phenomenon. Death-scapes have emerged in such faraway places as Bosnia, Chechnya, Palestine, Colombia, Sri Lanka, or Kashmir. Recent US-led wars in Iraq or in the Balkans can be characterized as such. Another configuration of terror and violence is embodied in a set of economic policies fostered by international financial institutions such as the World Bank and the IMF. The implementation of such policies in the absence of a significant reduction of African debt has led to the "spectralization" of the economies of the continent, as evidenced by the growth of casinos and gambling activities. Millions of people have been deprived of jobs, food and shelter and are now reduced to struggling for daily survival. Instead of curbing the corruption of local elites, the brutality of the international system has increased their greed and carelessness. Under the pretext of privatization, looting has become a norm as well as a cultural practice. Partial democratization under conditions of structural adjustment has opened the way for the privatization of violence.

*Under which conditions could a positive transition successfully be effected?*

Successful transition can only be effected under conditions of sustained economic growth and cultural aggiornamento. The current dilemma is how to unleash such a cycle of growth. I imagine that for this to happen, wars have to end. Internal frontiers have to be erased. Massive investments are needed in the fields of infrastructure, education and health. Transnational global connections have to be harnessed.

But economic growth alone will not be enough. It should be accompanied by a serious shift in the terms of cultural rendition of contemporary African experiences. People, images and commodities have to circulate. A continental public sphere has to be nurtured through the development of mass media and new technologies. A renewal of the virtue of intellectual curiosity has to replace the current syndrome of victimization. Bridges have to be built between a new social science and the various domains of the humanities, including philosophy, the arts, music, architecture, film and design. Such would be some of the attributes of an Afro-cosmopolitanism firmly rooted in the continent, but mindful of the force and wealth Africa's multiple internal and external diasporas represent.[4]

*Recently, you have spoken out against the still widespread "cult" or "neurosis of victimization" with respect to the aftermath of colonialism. What kind, if any, of cosmopolitanism could be the proper remedy against this neurosis?*

This is a difficult issue. We cannot evade the violent aspects of our history. We have to confront in the same breath the terror visited upon us by racial imperialism as well as our own self-inflicted brutalities. For this to happen, we have to widen the scope of cultural and political critique and renew the archives of our past and of our present.

But there is no way we will overcome the neurosis of victimization if, by transforming the past into our subjective present, we root our identities in injury alone. For the past to become a principle of action in the present, we have to manage to admit the reality of loss and stop living in the past instead of integrating it in to the present as that which must sustain human dialogue. In any case, the complete restitution of the past is not only terrifying, but also a clear impossibility.

In order to build a truly cosmopolitan culture in Africa, the present has somewhat to be liberated from the past. It should be clear that I am not advocating the erasure of the past. I am preoccupied with ways in which we can open avenues for memorial practices that foster the work of remembrance—but remembrance as part of the work of freedom, the ultimate ethical frontier. This cannot be achieved through black racial romanticism.

[1] Mbembe is referring to "Afro-centrist" discourses here, i.e. discourses that consider ethnicity as linked to a certain intellectual privilege (cf. the concepts of "négritude" or "Pan-Africanism"); see Achille Mbembe, "African Modes of Self-Writing," p. 252 ff.

[2] See Mbembe's groundbreaking essay "Provisional Notes on the Postcolony," in *Africa* 62, 1 (1992), reworked as "The Aesthetics of Vulgarity," in Achille Mbembe, *On the Postcolony*, p. 102-141.

[3] Achille Mbembe, "Necropolitics," in *Public Culture* 15, 1 (2003), p. 11–40.

[4] For a further elaboration on these topics, see for instance Achille Mbembe's recent essay on Johannesburg, "Aesthetics of Superfluity," in *Public Culture* 16, 3 (2004), p. 373–405.

# *Between Babel and Babylon* Conversation with Ella Shohat

Interview conducted in December 2006.

Ella Shohat is a rare example of an intellectual whose theoretical work has developed in close relation to her personal history and maintained an intricate connection to it throughout a huge variety of transdisciplinary projects. Being raised in Israel by Baghdadi parents, and speaking Arabic at home, she later moved to the United States to pursue her studies, experiencing yet another dimension of being out of place, an out-of-placeness that has been manifold. This existential factor of never quite belonging where you are set, both personally and with respect to a chosen discipline, informs her prolific work, which spans a large spectrum ranging from film/media studies, literary theory, and visual culture, to Middle Eastern, Jewish and postcolonial studies. From her early critique of Zionist discourse as articulated through the history of Israeli cinema and through her deconstructive analysis of Eurocentric thinking—carried out with her frequent collaborator, Robert Stam—to the re-formulation of the project of "critical polycentric multiculturalism" and "diasporic perspectives," Shohat's intellectual orientation has always been one of dismantling existing power structures and hierarchies. Not only does her work reveal the extent to which today's transnationalism and multiculturalism necessitate new modes of thinking, but it also emphasizes the complexity and sometimes contradictory nature of diasporic voices, which are seldom articulated with such clarity and rigor.

CH *A significant part of your writing is centered on concepts of displacement and exile. Can you briefly sketch how this concern came about, and especially how your own biography figures in the theoretical exploration of being out of place?*

ES I was born into a situation of displacement: my parents were dislocated from Iraq and did not exactly find a home in Israel, a traumatic moment of rupture that, to an extent, has shaped my perspective on questions of belonging Colonialism, on the one hand, and the rise of nationalism, on the other, have had disastrous consequences for diverse minorities. Given the violent geopolitics of the region, communities were uprooted overnight. Due to the Arab-Israeli conflict, my family was ejected from Baghdad, where our ancestors had lived for millennia. In Israel, partly because my parents' culture was that of the enemy, my family felt out of place. My parents used to say: "In Iraq we were Jews, and in Israel we are Arabs."

Our Arab culture was taboo. Yet, even if we tried, we could not easily escape the mark of otherness. It was written all over our bodies, looks, accents. My parents did not dare put the Arabic name they had given me, Habiba, on my Israeli birth-certificate. My grandparents continued to communicate only in Arabic for decades after their dislocation, until they passed away. For years, I was their everyday translator. I was raised among people who felt a great sense of loss because of the sudden move out of Iraq. Their powerlessness only added to their sense of alienation. But what was rather anomalous about this situation was that we were expected to define this exilic condition as a natural home and refuge. In my own writing I described this feeling by inverting the biblical phrase—"by the waters of the Zion, we laid down and wept when we remembered Babylon." My writing in this sense attempted to give a voice to this rupture, permitting, as it were, the mourning and melancholia that were so taboo for the dislocated Arab-Jews in Israel.

Being raised between Arabic and Hebrew was far from being a situation of happy bilingualism. It was a conflictual linguistic experience, where my school language was at war with my home language, which we were expected to forget and erase. This schism nourished my fantasies of an elsewhere. Israel may have been a land of many immigrants and displaced people, but it was not a multicultural democracy. It was a centralized nation-state dominated by the ideology of modernization that permitted only Eurocentric narratives of belonging. Israel was also a place where you could only take a boat or a plane in one direction—to the West—so perhaps it is no wonder that my fantasies centered on the United States, around the English language and Anglo-American culture. Anglo-American culture became a kind of a third space for me, an imaginary homeland, which transcended my own two languages. But the phantasmatic space of "America," often associated with the Hollywood dream-factory and the American Dream, was for me associated with the 1960s. It was rather ironic that I arrived in the conservative Reagan era.

*In what ways have travelling and moving out of the Middle East affected your experience and writing?*

I should first note that a visit to Europe in the mid-1970s preceded my move to New York. I was part of an art delegation funded by the Adenauer Foundation to encourage encounters between German and Israeli youth. We lived for a month in a little village, Hochspeyer, and as far as I can recall, I was the only Israeli of Iraqi origin, the only one who did not have direct European ancestry (although I was intimately exposed to European-Jews through a few intermarriages in the family; my aunt married a German Jew from Berlin, who moved to Israel at the end of the war). Toward the end, we all, the Israelis and the Germans, were taken to visit a not-so-well-known concentration/labour camp, Natzweiler, in Alsace-Lorraine. Although it was not used for mass extermination, some Jews and Gypsies were murdered in the gas chamber, often after serving as "anatomical specimens" for the medical school of Strasbourg University. The white porcelain surfaces and the shiny metal tools remained neatly displayed in the experiment room. And one could mentally animate the empty room with sights and sounds of scientific torture. The organized pile of shoes had been left as it was, we were told, since the day the camp was liberated. We were taken on a tour of the productivity of the system—the showers the Germans took daily ware fuelled by the busy crematorium. These are some of the nightmarish images that are part and parcel of my growing-up.

That tour of horror took place only a few years after the Munich massacre (1972), which was also lurking in the background of the Natzweiler experience. As was the rule, our delegation travelled with a 24-hour security person. We were there with German friends staring at the bad German, who was now fixed in history; but it was the bad Arab that had long passed the threshold to occupy a permanent seat in the Israeli national consciousness. Or so we were taught to believe. As an Arab-Jew, such a discourse presented a clear moral dualism of having to choose between the Jew and the Arab. But having an Iraqi memory perhaps made me uneasy about such false options and disturbing linkages, even back then. Later, the Natzweiler experience would endow me with the confidence to resist the hideous equation between Nazis and Arabs—a discourse that you can easily find in popular Israeli discourse. This is precisely the kind of associative images I ended up discussing in my book *Israeli Cinema: East/West and the Politics of Representation.*[1]

One central argument in my work on Zionist discourse concerned this rather paradoxical East/West imaginary. The West is viewed ambivalently, both as the historic crime scene of anti-Semitism and as an object of desire, an authoritative norm to be emulated in the East. It is as though the *Ostjuden* could only transform himself in the image of the West once he became a Jew in the (other, more Eastern) East; and let's not forget that the image of the New Jew, the Sabra, was projected as a muscular body working the land, often with blond hair and blue eyes. Palestine/Eretz Israel was also viewed ambivalently—the East, associated on the one hand with backwardness and underdevelopment, is associated on the other with oasis and solace—a return to geographical origins and reunification with the biblical past. Yet, in all these narratives the Palestinian was superfluous, irrelevant to the project of the Jewish "return into history."

## Displacement and Multiple Belonging

*So I guess the discovery of a third space or "elsewhere" did not stop at the imaginary or intellectual level … it became a reality.*

Traveling elsewhere became a mode of thinking of oneself "in" the world, not merely existing as a detached observer. I guess I gradually came to feel that being-at-home-in-the-world was less about a physical homeland than about participating in a community, a process of sharing ideas, wishes, hopes. There is a certain tension in my thought, almost opposite impulses, between a fundamental critique of the very idea of nation-state and the real-politic that begs committed intellectuals to address its privileges and discrepancies. Does the situation of stateless refugees and dislocated laborers suggest that we fight for citizenship rights or for undoing the nation-state idea? Where would transnational capital and the ideology of productivity figure in either theory?

Even in a globalized world, where we are all connected, border-crossing can be an act of self-fulfillment as much as it can be an act of desperation. Not all movements across borders are the same, and in all cases the question of "free choice" is complicated by economics, geopolitics, ideologies, etc. My family left Baghdad in a rush, having to renounce their citizenship (known as *Al-Tasqit*), forced to leave to Israel via Cyprus on a *laissez-passer* document—fearing to stay in Iraq but later mourning the impossibility of return. Did they really want to leave? Did they have any say in their dislocation? Could they choose to return? This situation was quite different from my own move to New York, and yet, can it simply be said that my move was only of my own making? Was New York an over-determined space for my initial way out of the schism between Hebrew and Arabic? One could argue that my move signifies that the effort to socialize me into the idea of "Zion" as my homeland failed, and that I found myself gravitating back toward the "Diaspora" experience discredited by Zionists, which in my case echoes an appropriate nominal geography—a new Babylon.

*In what ways was migrating to New York a liberating experience, and what did it mean to belong to America?*

I am not exactly sure what it means to belong to "America." It seems to me that because of the specific history of the Americas, one finds a dense space of diasporas, a palimpsest of displaced people who belong, simultaneously, to many places, and thus one can have a feeling of belonging to the Babel of America. When I moved to New York, I found a place inhabited by diverse dislocated people. In this fragmented space, the idea of someone belonging to multiple geographies was not completely out of the norm But in any case, being at home for me could no longer be easily bounded by geography. Iraq was out of bounds, but I could meet Iraqis at the same time. The borders separating Arab and Jew felt like they were melting; since, at least on the surface, I no longer lived within a context of a state invested in the schism between the Arab and the Jew New York, in a strange way, afforded me a breathing space, a way out of a virtually schizophrenic existence. In Israel, Sephardim/Mizrahim were called "Blacks" (*Schwartzes* in Yiddish), and ended up actually reclaiming this term as a positive signifier. As a young girl, I learned about the Black Panthers in the United States, because the Israeli Black Panthers movement named itself after the American movement. I guess that, because of this history, when I arrived in New York I sensed an immediate affinity with the concerns and struggles of minorities/people of color.

At the same time, the question "Where are you from?" has never been easy for me. Which geography does the question assume—that of the nation-state, that of a regional culture, that of linguistic knowledges? I can never give a simple answer. When I say that my family is from Baghdad, and that they are also Jews, it startles many Americans. I usually have to go through the same detailed explanation about my origins. Given the widespread Arab-versus-Jew discourse, it has been difficult to inscribe the hyphen between the Arab and the Jew. It provoked me to write a series of critical essays on the subject, some of which explicitly address the problem of the erasure of the hyphen.[2] Over the years, I have received very moving letters from people of diverse backgrounds identifying with the story, or finding resonance with their own.

But I also experienced political harassment due to my critical stance toward Israel. My first book on *Israeli Cinema* (1989) was the subject of an attack in Israel that traveled into the American academic context. An article I wrote entitled "Sephardim in Israel: Zionism from the Standpoint of its Jewish Victims" (1988) partially dialogued with Edward Said's article entitled "Zionism from the Standpoint of its Victims" (1979).[3] My essay assumed much of the Palestinian critique, but it also tried to deconstruct the idea of a homogeneous "Jewish History" (with capital "H"). I felt that even critical discourses were, ironically, deploying inadvertently the axioms of Zionist historiography. I was hoping to create an intellectual space that would address Jewish histories in the plural, especially when the story of Jews within Islam and Christianity are so markedly different.

The re-evaluation of Eurocentric discourses was applicable to other fields of knowledge as well. When I moved to the United States, I had a Bachelor of Arts in Philosophy and Comparative Literature and I began my graduate studies. In the humanities, the dominant feminist discourse then was psychoanalytic. Within such a universalist methodology, race, class and national stratification were a priori irrelevant. When I wrote essays like "Gender and the Culture of Empire"[4] in the late 1980s, it was in part a response to the Eurocentric assumptions of feminist film and literary theory. My text proposed alternative methods for feminist analysis; for example, looking for submerged racial presence in all-white films; or examining discursive tropes of empire, such as Freud's notion of the "dark continent of female sexuality," which I tried to contextualize within archaeological and geographical discourses of empire. For this reason, I was especially fascinated by the work of Frantz Fanon, and the challenge he began to pose for the practices of psychoanalysis and psychiatry.[5]

## A Postcolonial Writing of Feminism

*The intersection of colonialism, race, gender and sexuality came to play a central role in your book* Talking Visions: Multiculturalism Feminism in a Transnational Age.[6] *Could you explain how this argument relates to the history of feminism?*

Feminism tends to be narrated in a linear fashion, beginning with women's fight to empower themselves in the West, which then spreads to the "backward" world. What this diffusionist, modernizing narrative elides is the struggle of the "other" women around the world for empowerment, whose story is written out of the story of feminism. I was trying to re-narrativize feminist history, to re-read the activism of Third World women, especially in anti-colonial struggles, as a kind of subterranean, unrecognized form of feminism, and as a legitimate part of feminist historiography, even if the activists themselves did not label their work as feminist. Colonized women had been deeply involved in anti-colonialist and anti-racist movements long before their dialogue with the "women's movement." In fact, it is often their activism, within anti-colonialist and anti-racist movements, that has led to their political engagement in feminism. But these types of anti-patriarchal, and even at times anti-heterosexist subversions within anti-colonial struggles, remain marginal to the feminist canon, because, unfortunately, one kind of feminism retains the power of naming and narrativizing. My point was that history and its representations have to acknowledge a more complex way of relaying space and temporality.

We have to challenge the multiple sites of narrating history— especially feminist history and anti-colonial history. The postcolonial, multicultural and transnational feminist critique has been re-narrativizing History with a capital H in a polycentric way, unthinking Eurocentric and phallocentric epistemologies. It is our responsibility as critical thinkers, artists and cultural activists to re-engage the hegemonic narrative by which aesthetics and history are taught, and create new ways of knowing. The point was to redefine what constitutes a legitimate object of study for feminism; to broaden its significations to include a variety of battles—a multi-axes frame of analysis. In this sense, the multicultural and transnational debate became quite central to the reading or re-reading of feminism.

*It appears that in a Eurocentric feminist perspective, women in so-called Third World countries are easily victimized in rather direct ways.*

Let's take the case of clitoridectomy, which has provoked an international debate over the cruelty of (non-European) cultures, over the denial of women's pleasure, over the notion that women are impure, over the exclusion of women from marriage if they don't practice it—and so forth. Yet, women actively participate in the initiation of younger women into clitoridectomy. And when women participate in what is seen as oppressive practices—how then should feminists "enter" the conversation?? The point is to first acknowledge the contradictions posed for feminist thought. The issue gets further complicated when the basis for human rights intervention and legal language for asylum ends up replicating colonial discourse. Women or gay refugees can apply for asylum as victims of the "barbaric" nature of their culture. The rescue of African women or gays by feminists and queers from the so-called underdeveloped world promotes the West as, once again, a civilizational space. Such a narrative elides the struggles of women in Kenya or Egypt who have been combating such practices; it elides the complexity of African cultures, which cannot be reduced to this practice. The problem, then, is not simply the practice, but what narrative we deploy to resist such practices. The challenge is to avoid the rescue fantasies —that take us back to colonial narratives of modernization. (I am reminded of the film *Around the World in 80 Days*, where the English man rescues an Indian princess from *sati*.) Today, it is sometimes feminists who, inadvertently, play the heroines of the civilizing mission. Implicit in this rescue narrative is the assumption that the West has overcome its own gender troubles. The book in the sense was a collective project that posed the question not simply whether we should or should not condemn a specific practice, but how to address such practices, how to represent them, and in what context and within which discourses. Feminist analysis is confronted with, and must situate practices within, interwoven local/global economical, social, political, and cultural contexts.

My introduction to *Talking Visions* also critiques the assumption of a certain feminist work about gender and colonialism—that patriarchy and homophobia have existed everywhere at all times. Such statements are ahistorical, and undermine other narratives. For instance, some Native American communities were marked by egalitarian structures and did not have patriarchal social organizing; in them, the question of gender/sexual identity was quite fluid. When colonizers arrived in the Americas, not only did they occupy indigenous land, they also imposed new patriarchal structures. Annette Jaimes in *Talking Visions* addresses this imposition; the colonizers would not negotiate with indigenous women, leaders of their communities; only with the men the colonizers selected as representatives.[7]

## The Trouble with Eurocentrism

*The critique of imperial discourse, among other things, led to the famous work you did together with Robert Stam,* Unthinking Eurocentrism.[8] *Let me first ask what is the relation between Eurocentrism and Europe?*

The concept of "Eurocentrism" is constantly misunderstood. "Eurocentrism" is not a synonym for "European." For us, it refers to Euro-derived hegemonies rooted in colonialism and imperialism. Eurocentrism is a monological way of looking at the world, one that embeds many arbitrary hierarchies. Europeans can be non-Eurocentric, and non-Europeans can be Eurocentric. It is not Eurocentric to love Proust, and to go to bed early reading *A la Recherche du Temps Perdu*—but it is Eurocentric to use Proust as a stick to beat up Zulus. It is not Eurocentric to teach the canon; it is Eurocentric not to notice that the Caribbean is "in" *The Tempest*, that Belgian colonialism is "in" *Heart of Darkness*, that the native American is "in" the Renaissance, that debates about Haiti are "in" the French revolution, and so forth.

"Eurocentrism" is also not a synonym for "racism." The term is falsely seen as a gotcha accusation, as when people respond to our work with the reverse "gotcha," expressed in endless variations on the following sentence: "While criticizing Eurocentrism, aren't you still being Eurocentric when … Aren't you still being inside the system you are criticizing?" Such formulations suggest that there is a simple binarism between the West and the Rest, when the whole thrust of our work argues for looking into the overlapping syncretisms that predate even modernity. We do not believe the world lines up easily into the bad Eurocentrics on one side and good non-Eurocentrics on the other. Identity and location do not preclude Eurocentrism. Even the Black Jacobins who abolished slavery in Haiti could be seen as Eurocentric. Eurocentrism is the discursive and mediatic air that we breathe. Our critique of Eurocentrism does not propose a nostalgic return to some pre-European mode of thought, nor a utopian projection of a post-European future; it is meant as a cognitive prod, a way of thinking within non-segregationist frameworks that would force critical projects into relational enunciations—where a kind of translational zone would be at the core of the critique. It is a way of seeing Europe and non-Europe, coloniality and modernity, East and West, South and North, as mutually imbricated and mutually constitutive within asymmetrical relations of power.

For us, the term "Eurocentrism" points to the ideological substratum common to colonialist, imperialist, and racist discourse; a substratum that still undergirds, permeates and organizes many contemporary discourses, practices and representations—even after the formal end of colonialism. While colonialist discourse explicitly justifies colonialist practices, Eurocentric discourse takes for granted and normalizes the hierarchical power relations generated by colonialism and imperialism, without necessarily even thematizing those issues directly. We argued that Eurocentrism's links to the colonizing process are obscured within a buried epistemology. Like phallocentrism, Eurocentrism can be an implicit or unconscious way of organizing the world into systems of knowledge around Europe.

*In what ways, then, did you link the question of Eurocentrism to the polemic around multiculturalism?*

The idea of "multiculturalism" does not mean simply the fact of "many cultures." The emergence of the multicultural critique in the 1980s in the US was a response to the hegemonic Western canon and the marginalization of what was then called "Third World" in the curriculum. In this sense, the multicultural critique was both a political and epistemological project. For us, the concept of "multiculturalism" had to be defined in relation to Eurocentrism. The caricature of multicultural scholarship as a naive celebration of the many cultures of the world, all dancing around the maypole, points to the ignorance about the hundreds of scholarly books performing legal, philosophical, historical, literary, or ethnographic investigation, and complicating the taken-for-granted production of knowledge. And many such writers, including ourselves, have also criticized certain versions of multiculturalism. But having said that, we need to be aware how the attacks on multiculturalism by right-wing and some Leftist intellectuals serve to reproduce Eurocentric premises and power. Ultimately, we can say that the heated debate over multiculturalism suggests that the term is a sliding signifier onto which conflicting anxieties and hopes are projected.

We proposed to see all the intellectual polemics about multiculturalism as just one skirmish in a larger conflict common to most countries in the "Black" (and we would add the "Red") "Atlantic." The US tremors are local manifestations of a much larger and longer seismic shift engendered by the three events that delegitimized the West as the "central culture of reference." We referred to the conjunction of events that dramatically reshaped conceptions of the world order, traditionally seen as moving toward a progressive telos with Europe in the lead. These events—World War II, the Holocaust, decolonization (and the echoing minority struggles in the "internal colonies" of the US)—simultaneously delegitimized European hegemony and affirmed the cultural and political rights of the non-European nations emerging from the yoke of colonialism. If the war, European fascism, and the Holocaust revealed in all their horror an *internal* sickness within Europe as a site of racism, anti-Semitism, and totalitarianism, the "Third World" independence struggles in Asia, Africa and Latin America revealed the *external* revolt of the colonized against European domination. (Again, we use "European" in the broad sense to mean Euro-hegemony in the world, including in the white-dominated colonial settler-states of the Americas, and especially in the United States.) Since then, the neocolonial constraints on independence, and the limitations of the anti-colonial project itself, have become more visible. At the same time, the aggressive "preventive war" policies of the Bush Administration have opened up a gap with a chastened and now relatively well-behaved Europe that sees itself more and more as a "not-US." Actually, in our new book, *Flagging Patriotism: Crises of Narcissism and Anti-Americanism*,[9] we examine these rather intricate continuities and discontinuities. We critique the abuse of the idea of patriotism for militaristic purposes by the US right-wing. We also score American exceptionalism and the Francophobia of the Right, while also pointing out the problems with culturalist (as opposed to political) forms of anti-Americanism in Europe, Latin America and the Middle East.

## Transatlantic Debates in Translation

*Can you tell us more about your recent work on the intellectual debates across the Atlantic?*

My current work with Robert Stam, for a book to be entitled *The Culture Wars in Translation*,[10] explores the various ways in which North American, Latin American (especially Brazilian) and European (especially French) intellectuals have formulated these debates over race, multiculturalism, etc. The debates, we argue, must be seen in transnational terms, within a relational framework that transcends the confines of single national geographies. Our specific goal is to develop a historicized, poly-chronotopic and relational approach by seeing the culture wars against the broader backdrop of the history of an Atlantic World shaped by the violent "encounter" between Europe and indigenous America, by the exploitation and transplanting of African labor, and by the evolving attempts to go beyond "master-race democracy" to full, participatory, polyphonic equality.

This project concerning the "traveling" of the multicultural debates began as a response to a pair of short polemical articles by the French social scientists Pierre Bourdieu and Loïc Wacquant. The first of the Bourdieu-Wacquant essays attacked what the authors called "American multiculturalism," equating it with neoliberalism, imperialism and US-led globalization.[11] The second essay, "On the Cunning of Imperial Reason,"[12] attacked globalization and multiculturalism in general, and American writing about Brazil in particular, specifically Michael Hanchard's analysis of the black liberation movement in Brazil. Hanchard's work, the two sociologists argued, imposed US racial binarist categories on the Brazilian situation, in what amounted to a "brutal ethnic intrusion." In a response essay,[13] we argued that the first essay's equation of multiculturalism with imperialism was simplistic and uninformed—the two authors seemed completely unaware of virtually all the relevant literature—and that the second essay misrepresented not only Hanchard's work but also the racial situation in Brazil and the state of scholarship on race both in Brazil and the United States. We also went out of our way to explain that we were not attacking Bourdieu's work in general, for which we have considerable respect. Rather than speaking ill of Bourdieu, we were speaking ill of his own ill-speaking about issues and projects about which he had very little knowledge—movements that, ironically, had some resonance with his own assaults on privilege and discrimination within France itself.

Our larger goal has been to forge a relational method for charting the transnational movement of ideas and debates across various cultural geographies and national borders. What often gets lost in these debates is the actual work, which thinks modernity through coloniality, and postmodernity through postcoloniality. This work flies under diverse names and rubrics—critical race theory, radical pedagogy, revisionist history, border theory, critical multiculturalism, subaltern studies, comparative diaspora studies, transnational feminism, postcolonial theory and so forth. But they all share a common element—a radically critical and transdisciplinary engagement with the legacies of colonialism, slavery, imperialism, racism and Eurocentrism. For us, what such projects have in common is various forms and paths to destabilize the naturalized, or even unconscious, norms of Eurocentric epistemology.

*Are you suggesting, then, that the current culture wars have a long history?*

The term "culture wars" does evoke the contemporary public venom, but we have suggested that it would be misleading to propose a beginning that is simply within our living memory. For us, the contemporary projects inherit and transform very old struggles going back at least five hundred years. The issues raised in contemporary debates were present, in germ and usually under different names, when indigenous people fought against European conquest or criticized European social systems, when Africans fought and critiqued enslavement, when Blacks in the diaspora fought and critiqued and theorized racism in those societies. The debates were present in the Sepúlveda/de las Casas "Controversia." (Recently this was staged almost verbatim in a play by Jean-Claude Carrière,[14] and is still hauntingly relevant to the present.) The debates were present when Enlightenment philosophers talked about "freedom" and "natural goodness" and the "master/slave dialectic." They were present when French revolutionaries debated slavery in the colonies, and when American revolutionaries debated the "federal ratio." The various positions for and against conquest, slavery, racism and imperialism have been present and available for a long time; contemporary debates form revised editions of those earlier debates, re-inflected and re-accentuated for new circumstances.

*How does the concept of translation figure in this cross-Atlantic debate?*

Some aspects of the US debates about race and multiculturalism and postcoloniality, at least in superficial terms, have circulated around parts of the world, intersecting with debates elsewhere. Although this dissemination is partly due to the global reach of the English language and of the American academy, it would be misleading to see these movements, as Bourdieu-Wacquant do, as simply American or to say that they originated in the United States and then traveled elsewhere. The very ideas that formed so-called "American multiculturalism" had already traveled back and forth between the United States and other geographies, where they were combined and indigenized within other spaces. The "Voyages of Discovery," colonialism, slavery, US imperialist policies, military interventions, expulsions, immigration and the brain drain brought a hybridized mix of peoples and ideas into the Anglo-American academe, so that the critique of Eurocentrism was impacted by many movements from elsewhere. It was impacted by the anti-colonialist discourse of Césaire, Fanon, Ho Chi Minh, Memmi, Cabral (associated with the "Third World"), by poststructuralism (associated with France), by subaltern studies (associated with India), by hegemony theory (associated with Gramsci), by dependency theory (associated with Latin America), and by radical pedagogy (associated with Paulo Freire in Brazil), and *Intercultaralidad* (associated with indigenous America). These debates cannot be contained, then, within rigid geographically bounded borders and terminologies; inside and outside is a false dichotomy. To put it in translinguistic terms—we argue that all cultural interlocution takes place on transnational territory.

Throughout *The Culture Wars in Translation* we are concerned with the ways that cultural and ideological debates move across borders; the ways that they are translated, both literally and figuratively. We ask what anxieties and hopes are provoked by words such as "race" and "multiculturality" and "postcoloniality" in diverse national, institutional, and discursive contexts. What happens in the movement of debates from one geographical space and cultural semantics into another? We try to identify the rubrics and keywords that multicultural and postcolonial work performed in diverse spaces. We focus on the ways the terms themselves shift their political and epistemological valence as they travel or as they become out of place. We examine how contemporary debates were anticipated by debates during the Renaissance and the Enlightenment. Intellectual arguments about cultural geographies are themselves shaped within specific sites, and the ways that national comparisons and contrasts are mobilized tell us something about the premises, or the anxieties and projections that come into play.

At a moment when we tend to think of ourselves as post-Marxist, postfeminist, post-nationalist, post the post and beyond the meta, when few binarisms remain undeconstructed—except for the binarist/non-binarist binarism itself—one is surprised to find traces of old nationalisms and shared prejudices. Sometimes these prejudices create strange bedfellows, such as when European Leftist intellectuals, for example, begin to sound like US right-wingers. Why does the left-of-center French newspaper *Libération*, in the mid-1990s, interview Dinesh d'Souza as the reigning expert on multiculturalism? What kind of secret sharing is going on here? What is the role of national exceptionalisms, narcissisms, disavowals? What is the role of the asymmetries of power in knowledge production and dissemination?

## Disciplines, Geography and the Rethinking of Boundaries

*So the project is very much geared toward revealing unrecognized narcissisms and nationalisms that seem to come back into play with a vengeance …*

Ideas no longer travel in caravels, they travel through cyberspace. Intellectuals no longer ride in carriages to the castles of kings, they jet-set to conferences, or teleconference in place. Cultural syncretism is not a new phenomenon, but with these new technologies, debates spread almost instantaneously, and knowledge is shaped within hybridized interlocutions. Intellectuals are located within nation-state(s), even if as exilic and dispossessed, even if having an uneasy relationship with the national. What we found fascinating is the ways that the national and even national narcissism enter Leftist debates—unconsciously through the back door—of those intellectuals who may be speaking on behalf of the universal. We are interested in the denial and the anxiety that takes places in the context of the attack on the critique of Eurocentrism. Intellectuals still form part of the process by which nations see themselves as qualitatively different from and in partial opposition to other nations; they historically define themselves with and against and through their neighbors and victims and enemies. The "fictive we" of the nation may create injuries and wounds for some intellectuals, exactly as the "we" affirms and secures identity for others—but that process is articulated through a specular play of self and other, of mimesis and alterity.

*The Culture Wars in Translation* reveals a partly phantasmatic encounter, often with right- and left-wing versions, between various nationalisms, narcissisms and exceptionalisms, each projecting its heroes and villains. Our project tries to call attention to the role of cultural and national narcissism in how intellectuals might invest their libidinal desire in the critique of the racism of other nations while sliding over the critique of their own. The vainglorious debates about "my society is less racist than yours" eerily echo the old "our slavery was more humane than yours" and "our colonialism is more enlightened than yours." This situation calls not only for a reflexivity about national narcissism but also for a transnational examination of the linked modes of institutional racism within diversely globalized spaces, all forming part of historically linked geographies.

*What role does hybridization play in a critical rethinking of traditional fields of knowledge? How does this complication of the issue of "the West versus the Rest" carry over to individual disciplines like art history?*

Within the discipline of art history, for example, art has traditionally meant Western art. Artwork from Asia, Africa and the Americas is viewed as the domain of the respective area studies, or of the field of anthropology. (Often the required languages for a PhD degree in art history tend to be English, French, German and Italian; even Spanish tends to be excluded, not to mention non-European languages.) As we know, art in the West is deeply linked to the idea of the individual artist's signature and to the museum as an institution. Art in many other parts of the world had a different kind of history; it was not segregated from everyday life or cultural practices, and formed an integral part of various cosmologies. As such, this kind of art could not be subsumed under the aura of "Art" (with a capital A) within the museum space. The term "artifact" signified objects that were inferior to Art, and therefore were displayed in separate sections or museums—folklore or natural history. Art history, as a field, is embedded in such distinctions. This terminological distinction is classed and raced, and has its origins in Eurocentric, capitalist-colonialist modes of seeing the world. Even the very idea of the museum has to be understood in the context of colonialism. The museum emerges in conjunction with transporting new exotic objects from the "discovered" continents of the Americas, Asia, and Africa. Categorizing and classifying this wealth of new objects were ways of mastering their foreignness, and defining the West vis-à-vis the rest. The ethnographic museum, the exposition, the circus and the fair—all exhibited objects, plants, animals and people from the colonized world. The ethnographic museum, such as the Musée de l'Homme in Paris or the Museum of Natural History in New York, has allotted a space for the "Other," signifying an inferior culture. In contrast, the art museum exhibited the subjecthood of the Western artist as an individual genius creator. In other words, the museum contains in its foundation an epistemological project, with a rather ambivalent genealogy.

I have also been concerned with the stageist discourse on the sequencing of the history of the arts and aesthetics. This field is framed around a linear meta-narrative: realism leads to modernism, which leads to postmodernism, where everything else is assumed to be pale copies of European originals; where the Rest (the non-West) follows the cultural innovations of the West, the so-called "advanced world." This temporality is totally questionable, since realism was not an aesthetic that was dominant in most parts of the world. The avant-garde rebellion against modernism has to be seen as a local European rebellion, rather than as a universal transformation. In fact, the "West and the Rest" were never as segregated as Eurocentrism suggests. Greece, Rome, Renaissance, Enlightenment, Modernism—are seen as the highpoints of Western civilization; but they can also be understood as moments of cultural syncretism. Aesthetic ideas have always traveled in multiple directions, in parallel fashion or crisscrossing each other. Think back for example to the Moorish influence on the poetry of courtly love, or the African influence on modernist paintings, or even the impact of Asian forms like Kabuki, or Balinese theater; or Picasso's encounter with African sculpture and the kind of aesthetic innovations that arose from this encounter. Even the notion of modernist avant-garde cannot be narrativized in a vacuum without taking into account all these kinds of cross-cultural dialogues. In my chapter "Sacred Word, Profane Image: Theologies of Adaptation" (in *Taboo Memories, Diasporic Voices*), I have elaborated on the paradoxes of mimesis when taking into account multiple geographies, especially as their encounter intensifies under the auspices of imperial culture. At the very same period when the European avant-garde was experimenting with breaking away from mimesis, colonial Western institutions were spreading institutionalized mimesis to the colonies as an artistically superior mode to the local aesthetics. Verism was genealogically linked to the discourse of modernization—a discourse shared by both imperialist and nationalist ideologies. As appendages to the modernization project, art schools were founded in cities like Istanbul, Alexandria and Beirut. Artists of the "Orient" were learning to disorient regional aesthetics by mimicking Western styles of mimesis. Figurative art signaled a world in transition, in contrast to the largely abstract art of Islam, now rendered "traditional," an obsolescent practice that would inevitably have to be abandoned in favour of the forces of progress. Within this melioristic meta-narrative, mimesis conveyed not merely learning a mode of artistic technique, but also the process of becoming conversant with the aesthetic and cultural norms of so-called Western modernity.

In this strange rendezvous between East and West, realistic aesthetics signified modernity; while non-figurative art was implicitly cast as archaic. But such an encounter generates some fascinating paradoxes. During the same period that the Orient was learning realism, the Occident was unlearning it. The ideology of political and economic modernization found its aesthetic corollary not in avant-garde modernism, but rather in realism. In the same period that the modernist avant-garde was rebelling against mimesis, opting for new modes of abstract, geometric and minimalist representation, Arab-Muslim aesthetic practices were moving toward mimesis as an integral part of modernity. The introduction of aesthetic modernization in the Middle East was done as though this geography existed in a different temporal stage of history, without links to its contemporaneous modernist experimentation with the new languages of Futurism, Surrealism and Cubism—even as, ironically, these Western movements were borrowing and dialoguing with diverse non-mimetic aesthetics. The so-called non-West has not only been cast out of the meta-narrative of art history, but also presented within a developmental discourse—seeming to always lag behind. But it is a whole other matter if we move beyond such segregationist intellectual paradigms, viewing cultures as heteroglossic, rather than hermetically sealed off from one another. In a sense, my scholarly project is to offer a multi-perspectival approach, a kind of a Cubist re-reading of the multi-directional travel of aesthetic ideas.

[1] Ella Shohat, *Israeli Cinema: East/West and the Politics of Representation*. Austin, Texas: University of Texas Press 1989.

[2] Some of these essays have come out recently in the collection Ella Shohat, *Taboo Memories, Diasporic Voices*. Durham/London: Duke University Press 2006.

[3] Ella Shohat, "Sephardim in Israel: Zionism from the Standpoint of its Jewish Victims," in *Social Text*, No. 19/20 (Autumn, 1988), p. 1–35; Edward W. Said, "Zionism from the Standpoint of Its Victims," in *Social Text*, No. 1 (Winter, 1979), p. 7–58. Both are reprinted in Anne McClintock, Aamir Mufti, Ella Shohat (eds.), *Dangerous Liaisons: Gender, Nation, and Postcolonial Perspectives*. Minneapolis: The University of Minnesota Press 1997.

[4] Ella Shohat, "Gender and the Culture of Empire: Toward a Feminist Ethnography of the Cinema," in *Quarterly Review of Film and Video* 131 (Spring 1991), p. 45–84. Also in *Taboo Memories, Diasporic Voices*.

[5] Cf. the chapter "Post-Fanon and the Colonial: A Situational Diagnosis," in *Taboo Memories, Diasporic Voices*.

[6] Ella Shohat (ed.), *Talking Visions: Multiculturalism Feminism in a Transnational Age*. Cambridge, Mass.: MIT Press 1999.

[7] Cf. M.A. Jaimes-Guerrero, "Savage Hegemony: From 'Endangered Species' to Feminist Indiginism," in *Talking Visions*, p. 413–439.

[8] Ella Shohat & Robert Stam, *Unthinking Eurocentrism: Multiculturalism and the Media*. London/New York: Routledge 1994.

[9] Ella Shohat & Robert Stam, *Flagging Patriotism: Crises of Narcissism and Anti-Americanism*. London/New York: Routledge 2006.

[10] *The Culture Wars in Translation*. Forthcoming.

[11] Pierre Bourdieu and Loïc Wacquant, "La nouvelle vulgate planétaire," in *Le Monde Diplomatique*, May 2000, p. 6–7, http://www.monde-diplomatique.fr/2000/05/BOURDIEU/13727.

[12] Pierre Bourdieu and Loïc Wacquant, "On the Cunning of Imperial Reason," in *Theory, Culture & Society*, 16/1 (1999), p. 41–58.

[13] Ella Shohat & Robert Stam, "French Intellectuals and the U.S. Culture Wars," in *Black Renaissance Noire*, Vol. 3, No. 2 (Spring 2001), p. 90–119.

[14] Jean-Claude Carrière, *The Controversy of Valladolid*. English version by Richard Nelson. New York: Dramatist's Play Service 2005.

CHAPTER III

# On Globalization

# *Geography of Inequality* Conversation with David Harvey

Interview conducted in February 2001.

Opening up spaces of hope. Finding transitions from local to global forms of action. Highlighting spheres of cultural articulation within the international set-up. That is about how one could sum up the agenda of David Harvey, the proponent of a critical geography and thus of a kind of globalization theory that stays firmly anchored in the ground of material facts. *Spaces of Hope** is also the title of one of Harvey's most recent books, in which he investigates the possible points of political reconciliation between the individual, working body and the fluid world of mobile capital. Only on the basis of an inventory of unequal geographical developments can an assessment be made of what steps of translation and mediation really have to take place. For Harvey, globalization does not mean the linear and homogenizing triumphal march of an ever more uniform culture, but a process that is always inscribing new differences in the landscape.

Here, Harvey continues on from the studies that he brought out a good fifteen years ago as the first theory of postmodernity based on economics (*The Condition of Postmodernity***). Whereas back then it was terms like flexible accumulation, time-space condensation and post-Fordism that helped to reveal the extent of the postmodern change, now it is the magic concept of "unequal geographical development." The mirror may be broken, but this does not mean that new facets do not constantly become visible in the fragments; or that cultural globalization is not conceivable as a countermeasure to the triumphal march of economy.

* David Harvey, *Spaces of Hope*. Berkeley, Los Angeles: University of California Press 2000.

** David Harvey, *The Condition of Postmodernity: An Enquiry into the Origins of Cultural Change*. Cambridge Mass., Oxford UK: Blackwell 1990.

Other publications by David Harvey:

- *The Limits to Capital.* Oxford: Blackwell 1982.
- *Justice, Nature and the Geography of Difference.* Cambridge Mass., Oxford UK: Blackwell 1996.
- *Spaces of Capital: Towards a Critical Geography.* New York/London: Routledge 2001.
- *Paris, Capital of Modernity.* New York/London: Routledge 2003.
- *The New Imperialism.* Oxford: Oxford University Press 2003.
- *A Brief History of Neoliberalism.* Oxford: Oxford University Press 2005.
- *Limits to Capital.* London/New York: Verso 2007.

CH *Globalized postmodernity—if there is such a "thing" or "condition"—has increasingly become coded in a variety of (media) images that seem radically incompatible with each other. Looking at recent media-scapes, one has the image of violent protesters in Seattle, Washington, Prague and so on, whereas at the same time, the image of a malled or themed "eternally peaceful" consumer heaven is becoming more and more emblematic. Or, to give another example, we have the picture of the favela next to the one of a gated community connected to the outside world via wireless technology. How can the historical-geographical materialism that you theoretically pursue contribute to understanding these current incompatibilities and contradictions?*

DH I worry a bit about using terms like "globalized postmodernity," in part because they are so vague they could connote almost anything, but also because they make it seem as if some magical processes are occurring in the ether that then descend to earth with profound but uncontrollable effects upon our life-world. The reason I work with historical-geographical materialism is to counter such terms with a conceptual apparatus that is better grounded in processes that are occurring around us in the here and now. My hope is that this will give us ways to think about changing our world in more enlightened and progressive directions. This does not mean I am against abstractions or theories, but I want theories that are close to our reality and which can help us change it. For example, I have worked extensively over the years on the rules that govern the growth and expansion of capital in the quest for profitable accumulation. These "rules" extend to perpetually re-shaping the geographies of economic activities through regional and urban developments, international flows of capital and labor, shifting patterns of industrial development, resource extraction and consumption. From my studies of these processes (theoretical and material) I have come up with what I think is a powerful generalization: capitalism produces a social and physical landscape in its own image that is contradictory to its own stable perpetuation.

It is contradictory in a double sense. First, since capital accumulation is founded on a class relation of inequality, it embeds that inequality in the landscape (in, for example, the sites of spectacular consumption versus the zones of chronic impoverishment or in the gated communities of affluence and imprisoned ghettos of despair). But in freezing class relations and the processes of class reproduction in the landscape in this way, it both produces zones of political opposition and reduces its own flexibilities and growth possibilities (where are the new spaces to absorb consumer goods, the educated labor forces to staff new production activities?). The perpetuation of capitalism requires that the class relation be reproduced through geographical inequalities at the same time as it needs to prevent the inequalities becoming too frozen and entrenched or so blatant as to become centers of oppositional power.

The second sense arises out of the need for capitalism to produce a certain spatial structure (of transport and communications links, for example) to permit space to be overcome ("the annihilation of space through time" as Marx so famously put it in the *Grundrisse*). But once you have built these spaces (of transport and communication links, of urban centers, etc.) then they are fixed. They absorb a lot of capital and have to be used fully if the capital is not to be devalued or destroyed. So capital which needs to move freely in space to find new opportunities for profit also has to remain within these fixed channels. Periodically that tension erupts into distinctive crises of, for example, massive deindustrialization of traditional production centers and the reorganization of the global system of cities, of regional inequalities, and the like. The geographical landscape needs to be both fixed and flexible (if not highly volatile) at the same time. In this way I get to understand some of the internal contradictions of capitalism as distinctively geographical contradictions.

*A special focus within much recent theorizing has been put on locality and local context. These notions have gained considerable importance, especially as a kind of determining frame of both (cultural, economic, social) production and consumption. Place, or locality, is being "appropriated" BOTH by nostalgic or even reactionary endeavors that see it as a kind of protecting refuge AND by more utopian approaches toward the re-building of organic communities. What do you think a more appropriate conception of place would have to look like, given the obvious shortcomings of the two above-mentioned (extreme) approaches?*

You are right that place has been the focus of nostalgic and often reactionary politics or of an impossible utopianism that seeks to isolate itself from the currents of political-economic change swirling around in contemporary capitalism. But it is also much more than that. I do not agree with the idea that the significance of place or of the local/regional has disappeared. Curiously, it has become in some respects more important under contemporary capitalism than before. First, the amount of fixed capital that now has to be embedded in the land if places are to be competitive under contemporary capitalism is simply too huge not to force a place- or regional-based politics into the forefront of the system. Urban "growth machines" and "regional alliances" are very powerful elements within international capitalism. Furthermore, places now have to make themselves attractive sites for migratory capital, which means they have to sell themselves in some way; and the political effects of that on urban cultures, renovations, gentrification, consumption, as well as upon conditions of labor and of life are extensive. The ease with which capital can now move makes small differences in profitability or attractiveness of places important. Lastly, capitalism is as much about monopoly as it is about competition (witness the extensive growth of monopoly powers in the recent era of supposedly open competition—a testimony to how right Marx was to suggest that the end point of all competition is monopoly and the fiercer the competition the faster monopoly arrives). There is always an element of monopoly about places, particularly with regard to the degree that they can establish unique qualities—hence the appeal to the uniqueness and authenticity of local cultures as a way to assure monopoly powers (there is no other place quite like this one ...). The point here is to see the contradiction between greater fluidity and mobility of capital on the one hand and the increasing significance of places, regions, and even national identities on the other.

## From Manchester to São Paulo

*Aspects of place and space have famously figured in your theory of postmodernity, which is prominently based, among other things, on the notion of "time-space compression" (as well as the flexible accumulation of capital).*[1] *More recently, you have started to transform and extend this approach toward a more encompassing view of globalization. By the latter, you mean the "process of production of uneven temporal and geographical developments."*[2] *What are the distinctive features of this conception and how, for instance, does this go beyond the version of postmodernity outlined about ten years ago?*

The relation of space to place is best approached by asking some prior questions. First, it is useful to distinguish between globalization as a condition, a process and a political project. The process has its roots somewhere and I think it is important to recognize the ways in which, say, inter-urban competition and inter-nation as well as inter-power block competition has operated within the process. As a political project it has largely been orchestrated by the military and economic power of the United States, particularly through US control of institutions of global governance such as the World Bank and the IMF. But it is always open for other territories to engage in the system and insert themselves into niches and perhaps even change its direction (much as the city states of Hong Kong and Singapore as well as some of the other newly industrializing countries did in the 1980s and 1990s). So uneven geographical development lies at the basis of the political project and of the process, but it is also an outcome of the political-economic struggles that ensue between different centers of capitalist development. And then, of course, the unevenness goes even further as capital accumulation opens up new terrains for resource extraction and economic development, disrupting indigenous ways of life, different social traditions and ecological conditions. So I would always want to see globalization not as an undifferentiated or unified process but as a geographically articulated patterning of global capitalist activities and relations.

*Very decisive elements of your conception of "globalization" are both its productive, process-like character and its dramatically differentiating function, leading to widening social gaps between (what Zygmunt Bauman, for instance, has called) "the vagabond and the tourist." Besides all sorts of localisms (of the varieties already touched upon), cosmopolitanism seems to be the only political agenda suited to the task of mitigating the drastic effects of "uneven temporal and geographical developments."[3] How could cosmopolitanism keep up with the radically de-centering and fragmenting consequences of contemporary globalization, or which version of cosmopolitanism could do so?*

It is important first to recognize that inequalities, fragmentations, and differences have always been a fundamental feature of capitalist development (consider how it looked in the nineteenth-century industrial city in Europe, for example). What is now new is the sheer scale of development. Political organizing in a city like São Paulo, with nearly twenty million people, is very different from, say, nineteenth-century Manchester, which was much more compact and had less than a million people. And while there have always been important issues surrounding immigrant groups (like the Irish in nineteenth-century Manchester), the problems which now arise because of the lack of cultural, religious and ethnic/racial homogeneity within the workforce are also of a different order (the Mahgrebians in Paris, the Turks in Germany, the Bangladeshis in Britain). So is there a political stance that can allow some unity of political purpose across these differentiations without squelching the differences?

Some argue that cosmopolitanism provides a way, but then it depends on what kind of cosmopolitanism. Gramsci, for example, objected strongly to the kind of cosmopolitanism favored by the Catholic Church, and Marx and Engels objected to the cosmopolitanism of the bourgeoisie's production and consumption system for the world market. So the task for progressive groups is to find a new cosmopolitan/internationalism that acknowledges scale problems, uneven geographical developments (making the idea of socialism radically different in Zimbabwe than in Sweden), as well as all the cultural, ethnic, religious, gender differences, while also recognizing that we have common interests around environmental issues, labor rights, legal protections against violence, and the like. It is a tall order, but not an impossible task.

*Uneven economic development in the last 20 to 30 years has led not only to the widening of differences across the globe but also to a dramatic fragmentation within one and the same locality, for instance a city space. As you point out, a consequence of this development is a radical "spatialization" or scattering of political issues as opposed to a possible unified temporalization of anti-hegemonic, anti-capitalist struggle: "The production of space [becomes] a constitutive moment within ... the dynamics of capital accumulation and class struggle."[4] How can such a spatialization ever be made productive for the latter task, which has always heavily relied on the moment of unification (forming a bloc) within one and the same space-time framework?*

Part of the political task is precisely to address the question of how the production of space (by which I mean territorial organization, transport and communications links, possibilities of mobility of both capital and labor, the construction of physical networks—such as the internet—and of social networks—such as the various diasporas) plays into political questions in both negative and positive ways. Consider, for example, the trend toward the construction of larger territorial aggregates such as the European Union, NAFTA and MERCOSUR. Should these be viewed only as advantageous to capital (as the Left critique of Maastricht suggested) or should we also look upon these as potentialities for the Left to develop a unified front across the different national spaces? I do not think the full potentialities of the latter position have been properly explored, in part because Maastricht clearly was such a pro-capitalistic agreement. But the trick here is not to try to suppress the significance of national traditions and differences, but to work with them creatively across these diverse spaces. Otherwise, Left politics falls back into pure defense of local advantages and at a certain point may become indistinguishable from the reactionary politics of, say, the Northern Italian Leagues.

*A key element within your elaboration of "spaces of hope" is finding new and politically empowering connections between processes of uneven development and the individual body as a sort of micro-scale basis of capital accumulation. In this respect, you particularly stress the "laboring body as a site of resistance."[5] Concerning the labor process, recent developments have led more and more to a flexibilization and casualization of work. Structures of employment are radically changing, giving rise to more "immaterial work" and resulting in more deregulated but also intensified exploitation structures. How can the laboring body—in the light of all these processes which seem to make it more and more replaceable, and which make work more and more incommensurable on a global scale—be thought of as a profound basis of resistance?*

The reason why I begin with the laboring body is precisely because this is where the pain of globalizing uneven geographical development is directly felt. Backache, the loss of dignity, the degraded conditions of labor and of health, form the starting point for political revolt. And it is precisely the way in which contemporary systems of labor treat the person as a fragment of themselves which lies at the fulcrum of contemporary alienation from what capitalism is all about. The flexibilization and casualization of work accentuates all this (though a reading of Marx's *Capital* suggests that we have been witnessing a return to nineteenth-century conditions rather than anything fundamentally new). The task of politically organizing a moving, casualized work force is difficult, but this does not mean that the laboring body is not exactly the right point to start. The effects of contemporary work processes on that body are felt everywhere.

## Social Utopias and Culture

*A famous battle-cry for the "new economy" has been the purported insight that there is "no alternative" to free-market neoliberalism.*

*Mapped onto the social cartography of recent developments, this could also be read descriptively as if there were no alternative to widening social gaps, uneven geographical developments, and increasing ecological impasses. It occurs as if this kind of "free-market utopianism" had left no viable space for alternative models. Against all this, you are trying to mobilize another strain of utopianism, one that is firmly grounded in a complex analysis of the status quo. What do the contours of such a grounded utopianism look like, and how exactly can it be anchored in the conditions of globalized postmodernity?*

One of the deepest contradictions of contemporary capitalism is the way it perpetually emphasizes the importance of choice but at the same time asserts that we have no alternative to the particular choices it is able to provide. One of the ways in which all talk of alternatives has been suppressed is through the rejection or denigration of all utopian schemes. I hold that all alternative visions must be utopian and that we should therefore think positively about that way of arguing. But this does not mean that anything goes. My own interest is constructing ways of thought that allow us to keep our feet on the ground in relation to what exists (this is the point of my historical-geographical materialism) at the same time as we have a vision of where we want to go (the kind of socio-ecological order we want to construct) and how we might get there. Since we start from a position of uneven geographical development, and since globalization is a geographically articulated patterning of global capitalist activities and relations, we have to insert our political projects into the contradictions and interstices of those processes in order to explode them and construct viable alternatives.

*Historically, there have been lots of versions of utopia and you particularly draw attention to spatial versions (for instance, in the quest for the ideal city up to the "new urbanism" of the nineties) as well as to process-oriented utopianisms (the most prominent of which being free-market liberalism itself). Considered geographically, lots of utopias have been implemented, ranging from modernist versions of the ideal, gridded city to bourgeois utopias of suburban gated communities and developers' utopias of themed and spectacle-based inner cities. What lessons can be learned from all these attempts at utopia implementation—especially when trying to construct a utopia that could challenge uneven (global) developments?*

I think a study of utopianism, theoretical as well as applied, reveals a great deal about how to construct alternatives as well some of the serious pitfalls. I think the first thing I noticed was the stark contrast between the utopias of spatial form (usually expressed as a design for the ideal city) and the utopias of social process (such as that free market liberalism will lead us to some promised land of a universal happy future, or even the Marxist dream that class struggle will lead us there). I think separating the two is fundamentally misguided and it is for that reason that it seems imperative to unite the spatial form/social process aspects of utopian thinking into some more unified vision. The second thing I noticed, particularly about the utopias of spatial form, is how they all seemed to work at a particular scale—the city or the local community. This, too, seems quite inappropriate to the conditions of capitalism in the world market and to offer very little in the way of alternative. So we need a utopian vision that acknowledges the importance of traditional ideas without being trapped within their confines.

*You favor a kind of dialectical utopianism which is firmly based on the spatio-temporal unmaking of inequalities, a certain universalization of basic rights and values of the laboring body. Not only must such an unmaking work across different geographical scales (from neighborhoods to regions and more global territories) but also across different "discursive theaters"[6] as you call them (from the personal via collectivities and mediating institutions to more global translations of commonality). Capitalism—by virtue of its very basic units of money and the commodity form—has managed to successfully work across all these scales and theaters, but the question arises whether the universalization of basic rights can ever succeed on a similarly wide-ranging scale? Put more provocatively: What role could (and does) capitalism itself play in such a universalization?*

A certain kind of utopian vision has been implicit in how capitalism works. It has powered much of US internationalism (where, believe it or not, the US continues to think of itself as a force for good in the world and capable of helping bring goodness and light to all) and is deeply present in the ideology of neoliberalism (as espoused by figures like Margaret Thatcher). And I think we can learn a great deal about how to construct an alternative utopian project to capitalism by careful study of how capitalism has itself succeeded in overcoming some of the barriers to implementation implicit in more traditional utopian schemes. But here, too, there are some serious contradictions within the capitalistic version—it does indeed hold out the ideals of universal progress, of well-being for all, of human rights and respect for the individual, but it cannot deliver on them. This provides a golden opportunity for those of us who are concerned with constructing alternatives, because we can turn capitalism's rhetoric and record back upon itself. But beyond that, an alternative utopian project must figure out how to link together possibilities at different scales, beginning with the laboring body and the way in which the personal is always political, moving through the levels of community and nation, to a global project in which universals are firmly delineated yet in a dialectical relationship to what individuals are about. In short, since we know that any universal statement about human rights is irrelevant if individuals do not instantiate it in the way the personal is political, then how do we reach across those scales in constructive ways? Again, this may be a tall order but it is not impossible. The first step is to recognize the nature of our task. Beyond that I do not have all the answers (nor should I) but there are attempts, as for example, in the recent World Social Forum held in Porto Alegre (in opposition to the World Economic Forum held in Davos) to wrestle with these issues.[7]

*My last question concerns the proper conception of* cultural *globalization. There are versions of it that view the increasing intermingling of cultures as just the upshot of global economic processes, thereby making such "penetrations" politically useless. Other approaches tend to attach big utopian potentials to the increasing hybridization and mutual "undermining" of previously separated cultural spheres. What would you consider the appropriate picture of (multi-)culturalism within the relentlessly productive time-spaces of globalization?*

I generally find myself at odds with much of the literature on multiculturalism and hybridity. I object to the latter term because it suggests a beginning point of purity (which is both incorrect and politically dangerous). I am suspicious of multiculturalism because it seems to me exactly the kind of rhetoric that fits into the whole world of globalization and uneven geographical development under capitalist domination (at its crudest it reduces multiculturalism to a choice of ethnic restaurants). There are some very serious questions arising in the cultural sphere that have not been clearly understood or addressed. Culture is not something that is fixed forever but a dynamic field of endeavors in which redefinitions and reconfigurations are perpetually taking place. To be sure, capitalists are often out to co-opt, appropriate or even construct ideals of originality, authenticity, and the uniqueness of local culture because this yields them a monopoly rent. But at the same time, cultural production is one arena which is hard to control. The dynamics of cultural evolution provide a powerful beginning point for political action. In many ways I see the cultural producers as potential allies in the struggle to define alternatives, even though I recognize how quickly capital seeks to co-opt them (consider how "radical music" gets commercialized and tamed in the US). But if the cultural producers can become more closely allied with an alternative political project then it is possible to have their talents mobilized for such progressive purposes. Perhaps we can even look forward to a world where progressive forces of culture appropriate the powers of capital rather than the other way round.

[1] David Harvey, *The Condition of Postmodernity: An Enquiry into the Origins of Cultural Change.* Cambridge Mass., Oxford UK: Blackwell 1990.
[2] David Harvey, *Spaces of Hope*, p. 60.
[3] Cf. David Harvey, "Cosmopolitanism and the Banality of Geographical Evils," in *Public Culture*, Vol. 12, Nr. 2 (2000), p. 529–564 , and Pheng Cheah, Bruce Robbins (eds.), *Cosmopolitics: Thinking and Feeling Beyond the Nation.* Minneapolis: University of Minnesota Press 1998.
[4] David Harvey, *Spaces of Hope*, p. 57.
[5] Ibid., p. 49 and 97 ff.
[6] Ibid., p. 234 ff.
[7] January 25 to 29, 2001, Porto Alegre, Brazil; www.forumsocialmundial.org.br.

# *Global China Shop* Conversation with Zygmunt Bauman

Interview conducted in May 2003.

*Liquid Modernity*, *Society Under Siege*, *Liquid Love*—these are some of the titles under which Zygmunt Bauman has been analyzing current social and cultural changes year after year.[1] Bauman, who was born in the Polish town of Poznan in 1925 and has been living in Leeds in England since 1971, was himself confronted early on in life by radical political changes and deracinations—something that led to his later interest in modernity and the Holocaust, among other things.[2] When, in 1968, he again became the victim of an anti-Semitic expulsion, this time from the Warsaw University, he settled in Israel for a time before taking up the offer of a chair at Leeds University, where he was Head of Sociology for a long period.[3]

Since then, Bauman's theoretical expositions, highly topical and analytical, have accompanied what he once called the "great transformation of our time": the steady disappearance of formerly stable social relationships, the increasing degree of individualization within Western culture, and finally, the way politics is being sidelined in more and more flagrant fashion from global arenas of power. Whereas, as early as 1998, Baumann already emphasized the "human consequences" of globalization,[4] his most recent works explore lines of development in the "society under siege" in ever greater detail.[5] One of these lines leads to the question of how best to counter the new, global structures of power, what form the path from the precarious status of mere "onlooker" to active intervention could take without there being even more destruction in the global china shop, and what a time OF, or FOR, action could look like.

[1] Cf. Zygmunt Bauman, *Liquid Modernity*. Cambridge/Oxford: Polity Press 2000; *The Individualized Society*. Cambridge/Oxford: Polity Press 2001; *Society Under Siege*. Cambridge/Oxford: Polity Press 2002; *Liquid Love*. Cambridge/Oxford: Polity Press 2003.

[2] Cf. Zygmunt Bauman, *Modernity and the Holocaust*. Cambridge/Oxford: Polity Press 1989.

[3] Cf. the biographical interview with Madeleine Bunting, "Passion and Pessimism," in *The Guardian*, April 5, 2003; http://books.guardian.co.uk/review/story/0,12084,929598,00.html.

[4] Cf. Zygmunt Bauman, *Globalization: The Human Consequences*. Cambridge/Oxford: Polity Press 1998.

[5] Cf. Zygmunt Bauman, *Society Under Siege*. Cambridge/Oxford: Polity Press 2002.

CH *Some of your most recent work is focused on the issue of "society under siege." You see contemporary society—Western societies in particular—as being under attack by two major forces that at first sight seem to be quite different and distant from each other: one is the major pressure "from above" commonly termed as globalization, the other one is a more and more fragmenting push from below, recognizable in the increasing diversity of individualized life-styles, or in short, "life politics," as you call this phenomenon. With respect to these two pressures, you also diagnose an increasing cleavage between them—an extending void in which the possibility of an emancipative, democratic politics seems to vanish. What affinities, if any, and what significant "disjunctures"*[1] *are there between the two forces that contribute to this picture, and what are their most dramatic effects on society?*

ZB Indeed, for a long stretch of modern history it seemed that power and politics were "natural partners" destined to marry and remain wedded "till death do them part" (more precisely, divorce would mean the demise of both—no partner would survive the death of its partner). Equally, the state in its specifically modern form of a "nation-state" was seen as the natural residence of the couple. No marital infidelity, let alone adultery, was tolerated: following Max Weber's hint, the state was an institution claiming a monopoly on coercion, and since the capacity to coerce was the defining feature of power and since politics was assumed to be in the last account about the accumulation, distribution and deployment of power, it followed that the monopoly in question won't be reached and preserved unless it is extended over the administration of power and politics. This model was never of course implemented in full—but it marked the horizon of the modern efforts to re-shape human togetherness and reposition it on a more solid and longer lasting, safer and rational basis. Striving toward that model was commonly described as the essence of the "civilizing process": the declared purpose and inner logic of all "modernization."

At present both partners are leaving their shared household or staying there, but only part time. Power evaporates upward from the state into the supra-state, the No-Man's-Land of global extraterritoriality, while politics drips and trickles down into the space of life-politics. The two processes are not just interconnected—they are inconceivable in separation, as they invigorate, accelerate and intensify each other's course. The less power is left in the house of the state, the less is expected from the fast weakening state organs by the political actors, and fewer political aims are realistically and with conviction addressed toward the state. The more the state is deserted by politics, the less it is able to hold whatever remains of its once sovereign powers, now free to go and eager to emancipate from vexing political controls. As a result, there is now a split between power free from politics and politics unsupported by power, with the half-empty house of the state in-between; one of its walls is threatened by demolition, the other by falling apart—hardly an attractive site for the power & politics cohabitation.

The global space is the realm of power free from political constraints. The individual life is the realm of politics with no power of self-assertion. One consequence is a sort of a global china shop wide open to any willing bull; the other—individual lives struggling in vain to resolve private problems and fight back the private risks into which public issues, once handled and tackled by the powerful state, have crumbled.

*With respect to the force of globalization, there seem to be two quite significant but apparently contradictory elements at work. On the one hand, one recognizes an increasingly "master-less world" in which all sovereignty appears more and more evacuated and in which, as you say, "everything may happen, but nothing can be done."*[2] *On the other hand, a new global rule seems to be establishing itself in the wake of "uneven globalization processes"*[3]*—one that seems to depend on progressive political fragmentation (of states, territories, etc.) as well as on the uninhibited enforcement of free trade. How are these two tendencies within globalization connected? Is there, in other words, a "systematic" pattern behind the "new global disorder"?*

Your description of the present predicament is flawless; I can hardly improve on your portrayal, which is exemplarily succinct but comprehensive. Indeed, the weaker are the political actors "down there," and the less consequential their comings and goings become, the less constrained the power players "up there" feel and the more eager they are to behave accordingly. And so a process reminiscent of Gregory Bateson's "schismogenetic chain" is set in operation: the more unscrupulous and arrogant one side of the confrontation is, the meeker and more submissive the other becomes—and its sorry look adds further to the audacity and insolence of the first, which presses the second into more servility yet—and so on and on, with no clear end in view.

One feature I would add however to your picture: the bullying—a notion that is not accidentally derived from the bull's habits. Increasingly deregulated and uninhibited free trade is the prime mover, purpose and outcome of the schismogenetic sequence—the principal cause of stripping the states of the resources and prerogatives they need to exercise an effective power; but the naked force of coercion, military might, capacity to maim and kill, must constantly be kept ready to use and periodically deployed (in the most spectacular way possible) to crush an occasional condensation of countervailing force before it turns heavy enough to break through the bossing/bootlicking chain. Discrepancies in military might, rather than the differences in economic potentials, are the main resource that allows global powers to go on successfully resisting the emergence of a planetary set of checks and balances, an expanded version of the equilibrating mechanism which used to sustain the mutually strengthening and mutually constraining interaction of power and politics at the level of nation-states.

All talk of a "global system" is, to say the least, grossly premature. The most striking feature of the new planetary disorder is precisely its non-system-ness. Social totalities can be sensibly described as "systems" (that is, regular, rule-obeying, "patterned" and so by and large predictable and in principle controllable) thanks to that checking-and-balancing impact of mutually attuned "subsystems"—political, military, economic, juridical, cultural (let us note that they can be called "subsystems" only if they are coordinated in such a way). On a planetary plane, however, some elements once integrated into the social systems of the nation-states are spectacularly absent, and such elements as are wholly or partly present are clearly out-of-joint, "going it alone" and acting at cross-purposes. There is no global culture, no global judiciary, no global law, whereas emergent global politics and the globally preached ethical principles of human coexistence go against the grain of everything that the globally acting economic forces and globally aiming military forces stand for.

## Involuntary Tourists

*Globalization is characterized, among other things, by the condition of extra-territoriality. Extra-territoriality is crucially based on the resource of mobility which is shared across the different social strata —from the power elites to impoverished refugees—but which is quite unequally distributed. In this regard, you speak of a certain structural "likeness" of global players and refugees, of "tourists and vagabonds."*[4] *How is this likeness to be understood as regards the increasing difference between the two extremes? And how can the significance of these two exemplary figures (the tourist and the vagabond) be assessed when—as you state—mobility is not an option for 98 per cent of the world population altogether?*

Likeness? Both extremes of the emergent global hierarchy are already on the move. In that, they differ sharply from the wide middle stratum, which they erode on both sides and prompt to daydream of joining the upper stratum (of global players and/or tourists), yet be haunted by the nightmare of falling into the bottom category (of vagabonds and/or refugees). Yes, the overwhelming majority of humankind continues to stay put, but as you know from elementary physics, any movement is always a "movement in relation to …"; an object "moves" when its distance from/to another object changes. When the "movement" concept is metaphorically transferred from the physical to social space, physical (or geographical) distances are replaced by "social distances" plotted in the "space" of social relations. In the social space you can move without taking a single step in the physical space —without ever bodily/physically leaving your home.

This will happen if someone transforms the web of connections and interaction which defines your place in the world. For instance, the company you worked for has been swallowed by another, went bankrupt or decided to "downsize," thereby making you redundant; or the skills that used to be the foundation of your social position and your self-esteem became obsolete; or the cause in which you inscribed your projected identity has faded or has been discredited; or the values you pursued have been publicly devalued; or the dividing line between proper and improper you learned to observe has been shifted and what you came to hold dear has been denigrated; or the imagined community which you considered your home and to which you believed you belonged has become impotent to support you or turned its back on you. If any of these things has happened, you would become a vagabond, an unwilling tourist—forced to look for sustenance elsewhere and to leave behind what you naively trusted to remain "your world" as long as you live or until "something better," more attractive and more promising, came about. And however secure your "placement in the world" may feel at the moment, you know that all this may happen, and that if it does, you won't be able to do much to avert the disaster, let alone fight back and reverse it.

However tiny the category of refugees/vagabonds may be, its impact is therefore much greater than its size would imply. Everybody may stumble, and bad luck delivers its blows at random, and so the vagabonds-by-the-decree-of-fate who you cannot avoid seeing around are vivid reminders of the plight that may befall you at any moment. This is, perhaps, why we dearly wish to "send them back home" or lock them up, to chase them away—out of sight and out of mind ...

There seems to be but one way to escape the fate of "unwilling tourists": to become a willing one ... Committing oneself firmly to one particular place means exposing yourself to enormous risk, making yourself a hostage to an unknown fate, inviting trouble. Is it not better to keep all ties loose, all engagements temporary, all emotional involvements shallow, all commitments short-term and instantaneously revocable—so that you can easily move on at the time of your choice to a place of your choice the moment the old place becomes too shaky for comfort? Given the facility with which inscrutable, uncontrolled and unpredictable forces of fate may "unfix" even the apparently foolproof "fixes," is it not better to resist "being fixed" in the first place—so that once the blow is aimed in your direction you are ready to forestall it or at least soften the blow and mitigate its consequences?

Being stretched between the poles of "global tourists" and vagabonds/refugees generates a steady mental pressure likely in the longer run to engrave its trace on all aspects of living—and most prominently on the shape of preferred life strategies and distribution of life concerns. One option conspicuously missing in that pressure is that of resisting the globalizing logic—since both extremes, the resented and the attractive one alike, convey the same message of unavoidable extraterritoriality. This is why the statistics of people in-travel and those admittedly sedentary and firmly settled may mislead. They are at best snapshots, recording a momentary state of affairs cut out from its dynamic setting. It gives no information about the trends, but above all is mute about the intentions, hopes, fears and mental strivings of people caught in the picture.

*In your approach to globalization, you compare contemporary global space (or the new kind of territory constituted by the "space of flows") to a "frontier-land."*[5] *In this contested territory, adversaries are constantly on the move, political coalitions are—as for instance Donald Rumsfeld famously put it—strategically shifting and only temporary, everything seems to be pretty much in flux. At the same time, this new global space is also characterized by more and more refugees set in motion by forced displacement, and accordingly, more and more refugee camps—developments that seem to terminate in the establishment of more rigid border regimes than ever. How to these two tendencies within the planetary frontier-land go together?*

They are phenomena generated on two opposite ends of the new global hierarchy, which is formed, marked and measured by the unequal distribution of mostly one freedom: freedom to move, freedom of mobility. Being free to move (in geographical space and in the "network of social relations" alike) is the most coveted and cherished value—since it is the essential currency in which one can purchase all other values, including security: physical and bodily security as much as the security of social position.

The most common strategy in the contemporary power struggles boils down to the removing one by one of the obstacles to one's own mobility and limiting as much as possible the movement of others, particularly the mobility undertaken on the others' own initiative—the "unauthorized" movements, "illegal" movements. These two ostensibly opposite attitudes to "moving freely" are in fact mutually complementary. They need each other, they supplement each other in the contemporary version of power struggle. No universally available quality could be a privilege, and without a selectively and sparsely offered quality there will be no deprivation—and it is the privileges and the deprivations that give meaning and purpose to power struggles.

The stake of power struggle at all times was the privilege of "getting it my way"—in opposition to others who were doomed to suffer a lot not of their choosing. And, at all times, to be powerful meant to have freedom to maneuver, freedom to make unexpected, irregular, extraordinary moves which, being erratic and capricious, constituted the element of uncertainty and unpredictability in the situation of others (making such moves, called "miracles," is in all religions the prerogative of gods); whereas powerlessness went together with fixity, with perpetual submission to a routine and the resulting monotony of conduct. The repetitive behavior of rule-obeying actors made them utterly predictable. Their regularity allowed the power-holders to treat them as a "constant," not a "variable" in the calculation of their own moves.

This universal feature of all power relations and power struggles is currently manifested primarily in the opposition between the freedom to come and go versus spatial confinement. "Freedom to come and go" permits the deployment of "hit-and-run" tactics, the delivery of unexpected (and so impossible to pre-empt) blows—as well as washing hands of their consequences. Both possibilities make the position of the "settled" (glebae adscripti, in fact) frail and permanently vulnerable. Mobility would not be a privilege and a formidable power resource were it not complemented by territorial fixity of the powerless.

In the eyes of the "locals" (of the settled populations that have no wish to move places but fear that because of the unfettered mobility of the powers-that-be they may be uprooted against their will), the migrants already uprooted elsewhere and trying now to penetrate their hermetically sealed borders are vivid embodiments of their own fears. The sheer presence of the migrants within the field of view may be a cause of insomnia; it makes dashing or placating one's own fears all that more difficult, as it bears an indisputable testimony to the awesome uprooting powers at loose. In addition, the homeless migrants, squeezed out of their domicile yet barred access to any other, are "sitting ducks"—easy targets for unloading the accumulated anxiety generated by the whirlwind of uncontrollable, seemingly blind and contingent transformations encapsulated in the idea of "globalization." They offer a sort of a safety valve through which the seething concoction of fear and anger can be, and is, channeled away from its genuine causes: that is, away from the forces operating at the other, unreachable and elusive, extreme of global hierarchy.

*With respect to globalization, you also state the end of "the era of space" and the rise of "the era of speed." You particularly view the events of September 11, 2001 as marking the "symbolic end of the era of space."*[6] *Concerning the long aftermath of these events (as we are now witnessing), it would be interesting to learn more about the overall "role" of terrorism in relation to this crucial shift (viz. the end of the era of space). On the one hand, territorial considerations may well have played an important role in the September 11 attacks (the selection of US landmarks, hitting the enemy on its own homeland, etc.). On the other hand, it was dramatically demonstrated (as you yourself analyze) that even the new power structure of (territorially unbound) speed and acceleration does not offer more immunity than the "old regime" of territorial solidity.*

"Free trade" which no local powers are able to stop or allowed to interfere with is meant to render physical occupation and administration of a territory unnecessary for the exploitation of its riches, and therefore eminently avoidable. That new opportunity is taken by the global powers with a sigh of relief; administration of the territory, running its daily affairs and servicing law and order is a chore—awkward and costly —that is better left to the minions ("Iraqis themselves," "Afghans themselves," or junior "partners of the coalition"). There are but few exceptions to that rule, like oil fields, notorious for their scarcity and exceptional vulnerability to terrorist blackmail, yet quite central to the "mode of life" which global powers wish to preserve as their privilege and in whose defense they wage their global wars.

The other point is that terrorism is extraterritorial, just like the global forces it assaults, and that territorial wars are for this reason largely irrelevant to its spread and activity —even if the general staffs of the globally acting armies would not admit it lest they seriously undermine their raison d'être. Terrorists are the least likely casualties of territorial wars: the self-proclaimed "anti-terrorist wars" destroy well-nigh everything except the terrorism, their declared targets. Having torn or frayed the web of social bonds supporting life routines, such wars make the assaulted territory more hospitable to terrorists than ever before.

Terrorism, just like other global forces, thrives on being non-localizable, "un-pinpoint-able," and on steering clear of the regular frontlines and battlefields. Its specialty is surprise: sporadic hit-and-run blows interspersed with intervals of invisibility. Its strength lies precisely in its knack of breaking the routine, in its ability to deliver blows unexpectedly and at places where they have been least expected. Terrorism comes very close to the model of "miracle-making," the notorious feature of the divine (or satanic, depending on the church to which one belongs) and of the sublime—the objects of, simultaneously, terror and fascination. Against such phenomenon, territorial actions are helpless. It is easier to find a needle in a haystack: unlike the terrorists, needles do not move and can be found exactly where they hurt.

Fighting for "security," understood as an insurance against the unexpected and once hoped to be brought to a victorious end by tightening the defensive city walls and digging deeper moats, is unwinnable in the post-spatial era. Its most tangible (perhaps the only tangible) effect today consists in lubricating the wheels of global forces, of which the terrorism is the alter ego, a copycat imitation or caricature. Terrorism is perhaps an unanticipated, but all the same inescapable consequence of extraterritoriality and the rule of speed. Another side effect is the spectacular growth of the "security industry," guaranteed a long and unstoppable progress thanks precisely to its ineffectiveness.

## Liquid Life

*In recent years, you have famously outlined the conditions of modernity in its contemporary "liquid" phase, as opposed to modernity in its previous solid state.*[7] *Among these conditions is the fact that power has been increasingly "evacuated from politics" and that "traditional" politics has been increasingly channeled into the domain of "life politics"—"the consummately individual pursuit," as you say. It seems that liquid modernity has, besides all other irreversible effects on society, led to an almost total emptying out of Politics (with a capital "P"). Against this, we have seen a proliferation of political issues, new political subjects, demands for identity recognition, manifold claims for a radical and plural democracy, and so on, over the past decades. Can you comment?*

We have discussed already, however briefly, the divorce between power and politics, with both divorcees moving away from the once shared home of the nation-state. I cannot add much to what we've talked about so far. It is obvious that bringing power and politics once more together is one of the most urgent (and awesome) challenges of our times, truly a matter of life and death for the planet we share—but where they will settle to live together is a wide-open question, which can be answered only through historical action, and after passing a long string of trials and errors. Perhaps we lack even the terms in which we could speak of their future cohabitation and interaction. People who were instrumental in the creation of the modern state and in the invention of representative democracy as the device tying power to politics had just the memory of the ancient city-based democracy as the only source of inspiration—but no preconceived view of how it could be "updated" to new conditions and raised to the level of an "imagined community." State-centered modern democracy was not a blow-up replica of ancient democracy, and it is very unlikely that the future "global democracy" will be a magnified copy of the parliamentary institutions which we came to view as the sole form the democratic control over power can take. All such institutions have been cut to the measure of intentions and possibilities of a territorially confined nation-state and can hardly be inflated to embrace a quite different, inherently multi-ethnic, multi-cultural planetary "totality."

To make the task of guessing the future shape of planetary democracy yet more difficult, none of the most prominent actors of the global stage seems likely to be among its promoters. Nation-states, under the pressure of their own democratic institutions, naturally focus on what separates their citizenry from the world on the other side of the state borders, not on what unites them with the rest of mankind. They tend to articulate "our interests," unique and different, and therefore standing in the way of the sharing, caring, full-blown across-borders solidarity which must be a necessary, even if not sufficient, condition of the kind of "allgemeine Vereinigung" which according to Kant is the ultimate and inescapable destination of the inhabitants of the planet. Global forces are free from such restrictions (along with all other democratic restraints)—but they can only rejoice in the resulting fragmentation of the political stage, since the mutual estrangement of the existing political units makes their free roaming of the planet much easier. The effective actors of the emergent planetary politics will therefore need to appear outside the currently recognized web of political institutions—in places and forms heretofore unknown. Perhaps such actors are already here, but blinded as we are by the orthodox concepts of politics and democracy, we fail to spot them and acknowledge their importance.

*Most recently, you have extended the account of liquid modernity to personal bonds and relationships, to the bases of all togetherness and community, so to speak. It seems as if these bonds are marked by an ever more short-termed, provisional, "until further notice" character that creates more and more ego-centered precariousness. Are the "liquification" of modernity and the all-increasing individualization of society just two sides of one and the same coin, or, to put it differently, what other crucial scenarios might the liquification process include and/or generate besides an enforced individualization?*

Numerous power issues are currently free-floating, let out of political frames; and plenty of political concerns and actions are desperately seeking power supports. No longer cemented by marital vows, power and politics, each on its own, experiment with "one-night stands" and "trial cohabitations." Just like in individual life, full of "semi-detached," "fixed term," "rolling contracts" of "long-distance" couplings, which I tried to put on record in my recent book on *Liquid Love.*

The many forms which political activity puts on and takes off while moving from one episode to another, one issue to another, one cause to another, need to be closely watched as potential signals of the realities to come; in my view, however, it is much too early to attempt final verdicts on their significance. It is particularly hard to set apart in a credible fashion the vociferously promoted yet fast fading fads from the considerably less dramatic and spectacular, yet much more durable and seminal gambits. Historians writing in the middle of the current century will be in a better position than we are to tell which headline-hitting political events of our time were no more than doomed attempts to hark back to a non-restorable past, and which of the comparatively innocuous and unpromising initiatives, dismissed as "senseless," "irrational," and above all "marginal," were pregnant with a long and distinguished history.

But the search for new meeting points for politics and power has already started; it is ongoing and in all probability will intensify. There is a void waiting to be filled, and there are prospective actors to fill it, though neither the observers nor the actors themselves know yet for sure who they are or how their role in a "new synthesis" will be eventually played.

Thus far it looks as if a further fragmentation of agents was unstoppable. It seems to be unstoppable partly because, when thinking about the present state of affairs and its prospects, we tend, consciously or not but quite naturally, to start out from present-day trends, taking them for "objective reality" and manifestations of some sort of "historical inevitability"—forgetting that they are but outcomes of our past practices. We tend to start from a humanity split into mutually suspicious, quarrelling, militant, pugnacious and hostile units—ethnic, religious, cultural and what not—and then stretch our minds to consider how all such warring factions could be brought together and forced or convinced to forget or at least suspend their differences and enmities and agree to live together in peace in spite of them. This seems then a truly Herculean task …

We may however look at the present plight from the other end: starting from our shared humanity. In our "global information age" we know of each other's conditions more than our ancestors ever knew about theirs. We have more opportunity than ever to experience and feel our common humanity. We watch the scenes of far-away atrocities and miseries and we cannot fail to notice that a maimed or famished child is a maimed or famished child wherever and in whichever way it was maimed or brought to famine, that the sorrows of a bereaved mother, widowed wife or orphaned children are awesome and tragic in every place, in every ethnic and religious community, that the pains of humiliation, rejection, exclusion are painful everywhere and for whatever reason they are suffered. In short, we know that underneath all these squabbles and hostilities lies the essential similarity of human beings and that the human way of being in the world posits similar challenges in every nook and cranny of the planet. So how come, despite the underlying unity of needs and purposes, despite the fundamental solidarity of human condition, we bring ourselves to act in a fashion that looks like, and can be credibly presented, as a proof of our incompatibility? Surely, splits and more splits are not the only direction in which we can move?

## The Power of Surfing

*As regards the "Great Transformation of our time,"[7] you also speak of new techniques of power that include, among other things, control through insecurity and uncertainty. You claim that the model of Bentham's Panopticon does not seem to be adequate vis-à-vis the new realities (especially flexibilized, bottom-up labor realities) anymore. At the same time, you also see a "New Big Brother" at work, especially in today's media-scapes. How can these two moments be integrated within a common model of the new power techniques? What other tenets should it be based upon?*

Well observed, but wrongly interpreted, I think ... Yes, that "Big Brother that is always watching you" is alive and well. He is also armed with telescopes and microscopes and cameras of which his Orwellian original could only dream (if, that is, he had enough imagination). But he is not the same Big Brother that the Orwellian original was, and he does not share his interests. To put it in a nutshell: the original Big Brother watched people to keep them in, whereas his present-day successor watches them to keep them out.

The old Big Brother was preoccupied with inclusion—integration, getting people into line and keeping them there. The new Big Brother's concern is exclusion—spotting the people who do not fit into the place they are in, banishing them from there and deporting them to "where they came from" or "where they belong," and better still never allowing them to come anywhere near in the first place. The new Big Brother supplies the immigration officers with the lists of people they should not let in, and bankers with the list of people they should not let into the company of the credit-worthy. He instructs the guards whom they should stop at the gate and not let inside the gated community. He inspires the neighborhood-watchers to spy out and kick out the suspected prowlers and loiterers—strangers out of place. He offers the homeowners closed-circuit television to keep the undesirables out of the door. He is the patron saint of all bouncers, whether in the service of a nightclub or of a State Ministry of Home Affairs.

Of course, the news of the decease of the old-style Big Brother would be, as Mark Twain famously pointed out, grossly exaggerated. Both Big Brothers—old and new—sit next to each other in the passport control booths at the airports, only the new one scrupulously checks the travel documents on arrival, whereas the old one checks them, rather perfunctorily, on departure.

The old Big Brother is alive and equipped better than ever—but he is now to be found mostly in the off-limits, marginalized parts of social space like urban ghettoes, refugee camps or prisons. There, the old task remains of keeping people in and bringing them in line whenever they fall out. As a hundred years ago, that Big Brother is the patron saint of all varieties of jailers. This is, you may say, an important role—and a role which, because of being kept in the limelight and widely advertised, is commonly alleged to be even more important than it is. But it is now a secondary, derivative, supplementary role to that played by the new-style Big Brother; its true task is to make the new Big Brother's task a bit easier. Between themselves, the two brothers police and service the borderline between the "inside" and the "outside." Their respective scopes of work swell together, depending on the sensitivity, porosity and vulnerability of borders.

Together, they embrace the whole of the social universe. You can move only from the sovereign realm of one Big Brother into the estate of the other—and one of the old-style Big Brother's functions is to make you see the otherwise vexing attention of his younger sibling as a life-saving operation and a warrant of a secure and blissful existence.

Aware of the ways and means of the old Big Brother, you would thank God for putting you under the younger one's surveillance …

*Especially telling about contemporary "liquid life politics" appears to be the metaphor of surfing, which applies not only to the navigational modus of and within global media, but also to social positioning: surfing the networks, surfing through power hierarchies, gliding through liquid social and personal relationships. "The success of a surfer depends on the ability to stay on the surface,"*[8] *you state, implying that certain depth qualities have been lost in the process. Is this surf metaphor confined to the current power elites whose "safety might lie in their speed," or how far could it be generalized so as to include all social strata?*

As Jeremy Seabrook pointed out, rich and poor live in the same universe. I may add that, courtesy of the truly mass media, this fact can no longer be escaped. On our "information highway" the high and mighty are the leaders of the pack, pace setters, idols to applaud and the universally watched examples to follow or imitate. For every haute couture original, there are High Street mass-produced copies for mass consumption.

And so it is with "surfing"—at least the mass-produced replicas of the real stuff in the form of "virtual surfing": surfing through the electronic network with the help of mobile telephones and messaging … Unlike the old-fashioned habit of placing one's feet under the table, facing each other, engaging in long and hard negotiation of mutual right and duties, taking and acknowledging commitments and monitoring their loyal observance—an electronically operated "network," in which the facility to switch off, to disconnect, is as important, if not more, as easy connection. Asked by the researchers why he prefers "internet dating" to the now old-fashioned singles bars or discotheques, a young professional answered: "Because you can always press 'delete.'" Surfing allows you to connect without obligation, on the pattern of commodity promotion: "Return to shop if not satisfied," "Money-back guarantee." No need to dig deeper, to take risks, or above all to tie your hands for a long time to come; if satisfaction is not instant and effortless, you may always shift your attention elsewhere, where joys come quicker and their providers may be turned off whenever the supply thins out.

According to Gresham's law, inferior coins tend to push out of circulation the more valuable ones. The easy access to instant and risk-free, but shallow connections tends to elbow out of use the deeper, but more risky and more time-consuming orthodox relationships. "Virtual relationships" set the pattern which other inter-human relations are expected to follow; the latter are criticized and resented in cases where they fail to do so. I tried to analyze that phenomenon in *Liquid Love*, and then again in the chapter of *Wasted Lives* called "Culture of Waste."[9]

*Under the current conditions of increased global interdependency and incessant information exchange, you claim that we have all become "bystanders"—which of course leads to vexing ethical considerations as regards the role of "bystanders" vis-à-vis the manifold evils in the world.*[10] *Could you briefly sketch a possible trajectory from this—almost universally prescribed—bystander position to the more autonomous role of acting upon the causes and roots of such "evil?" In the case of the war on Iraq, for instance, there hardly seems to be another role imaginable than the one of a bystander in utter disbelief. In this case, going to the roots and causes (which have been analyzed over and over again), or even taking the issue to the streets (as millions did), was not really instrumental in creating such a new actor.*

You are quite right. The road from bystander to actor is perhaps the road most difficult today to negotiate and yet the one most urgently demanding to be negotiated. Luc Boltanski spelt out the intricacy of the challenge in his *Distant*

*Suffering*[11]—and I have little to add to his perceptive insights. How to plug the gap stretching between moral sentiments and ability to act effectively? This is the question to which our generation, for the sake of all future generations, needs to provide an answer.

[1] Cf. Arjun Appadurai, *Modernity at Large: Cultural Dimensions of Globalization*. Minneapolis/London: University of Minnesota Press 1996, p. 27 ff.
[2] Zygmunt Bauman, *Society Under Siege*, p. 18.
[3] Cf. David Harvey, *Spaces of Hope*. Berkeley/Los Angeles: University of California Press 2000, p. 60 ff., and the interview in this volume.
[4] Cf. Zygmunt Bauman, *Globalization: The Human Consequences*. Cambridge/Oxford: Polity Press 1998, p. 77 ff.
[5] Cf. Zygmunt Bauman, *Society Under Siege*, p. 90 ff. and *Liquid Love*, p. 135 f.
[6] Zygmunt Bauman, *Society Under Siege*, p. 87.
[7] Cf. Zygmunt Bauman, *Liquid Modernity*. Cambridge/Oxford: Polity Press 2000.
[8] Cf. Zygmunt Bauman, *Society Under Siege*, p. 52 ff.
[9] Zygmunt Bauman, *Wasted Lives*. Cambridge/Oxford: Polity Press 2004.
[10] Cf. Zygmunt Bauman, *Society Under Siege*, p. 201 ff.
[11] Luc Boltanski, *Distant Suffering: Morality, Media and Politics*. Cambridge/New York: Cambridge University Press 1999.

CHAPTER IV

# On Activism and Participation

# *Visible Invisible Violence* Conversation with Tariq Ali

Interview conducted in December 2005.

*Rough Music.** That is not just the title of Tariq Ali's book about the suicide attacks in London in July 2005. "Rough Music" is also what Ali has been deploying against imperial endeavors of every kind for over four decades. Born in Lahore (now in Pakistan) in 1943, the author and filmmaker has been living in London since the early 1960s. Ali was not only a leading light in the movement opposed to the Vietnam War. In the aftermath of September 11, 2001, he knew how to combine analysis and activism in an effective and relevant way. Since then, in a number of writings, he has sharply criticized the Western recolonization of Iraq and the Arab world.** Tariq Ali, whose extensive works also include the so-called "Islamic Quintet"—four volumes of fiction have been published to date***—, has been a co-editor of the *New Left Review* for several years. His last book, *The Dictatorship of Capital*, was published in 2008 by Verso.

* Tariq Ali, *Rough Music: Blair/Bombs/Baghdad/London/Terror.* London/New York: Verso 2005.

** See Tariq Ali, *The Clash of Fundamentalisms: Crusades, Jihads and Modernity.* London/New York: Verso 2002 and *Bush in Babylon: Recolonising Iraq.* London/New York: Verso 2003. An archive of Ali's publications is to be found at www.tariqali.org.

*** Tariq Ali, *Shadows of the Pomegranate Tree.* London/New York: Verso 1996, *The Book of Saladin.* London/New York: Verso 1998, *The Stone Woman.* London/New York: Verso 2000 and *A Sultan in Palermo.* London/New York: Verso 2005.

CH *There seems to be a particular kind of amnesia (at least in our Western minds and our public consciousness) about events related to the US-led occupation of Iraq. For instance, the number of civilian casualties remains pretty much unclear, or is maybe even deliberately obscured. There are estimates (like the one on www.iraqbodycount.org, or by certain human rights groups),*[1] *but as General Franks of the US Central Command has expressed it, "We don't do body counts"—something which is of course not true when it comes to the total number of American soldiers being killed. What do you see as the prime reasons for this crude disregard?*

TA "We don't do body-counts" is the voice of empires past and present: the Belgians in the Congo, the British in Kenya, the French in Algeria, the Germans in Namibia, the US in South America, Japan, Southeast Asia and now Iraq. The phrase refers, of course, to the bodies of those whose countries have been occupied. *Untermenschen.*

The crude racism that underlines most imperial occupations is evident. What is interesting in these "human rights" times, when Western citizens are supposed to be concerned with the loss of all human life, is that there is a casual disregard for the Iraqis who are being killed. The Western media is largely responsible for this with its selective reporting, its silences and its fear of offending the imperial power too much. Even in Germany there has been a sudden and sharp shift in the media—both newspapers (*SZ*, *FAZ*) and magazines like *Der Spiegel* and *Die Zeit*, and the TV stations (including *Arte* and *ZDF*)—and the space for dissenting voices have almost been completely curtailed. This is in sharp contrast to journals like the *New York Review of Books*, which has kept up a steady barrage against lies and torture, and the *London Review of Books*, whose coverage of Palestine has been exceptional. Both of these journals continue to defy the global trend.

*In a recent essay,[2] you ask (with respect to occupation endeavors in general and the torture at Abu Ghraib prison in particular) if "the citizens of North America have forgotten what happened in South and Central America, Asia, and Africa less than fifty years ago?" Is collective memory loss the result of an overall superiority complex (as you state in that essay), or what could be the more concrete—or perhaps the politically engineered—factors behind it?*

It is partially the parochialism of US society. It is such a large country that most of its citizens do not have a passport. They see no reason to travel elsewhere. They learn geography when their government invades a new country. Partially, it is also the cultural decline of the mainstream TV channels and the media in general. Globalization has produced a narrow culture everywhere, but nowhere as dramatically as in the United States. Despite this, reality often transcends the media bubble, as we can witness in Cindy Sheehan's campaign against the war, which wrong-footed the media and the Bush administration. When wars go badly, then there is dissent within the empire which overrides the lies of politicians and embedded journalists.

*Before the US occupation started, over eight million people took to the streets all over the world to air their protest against this unjustified and poorly argued endeavor. The governments that were most eager to go to war deliberately ignored and dismissed this protest movement, which was, at least in terms of its sheer size, unprecedented in history. What light does this shed on the democratic process in the very countries that present themselves as the "strongest" (or most violent) defenders of Western democratic values?*

Alas, the eight million who marched were ignored by an imperial leadership hell-bent on war, but they were also ignored by their representatives in parliament. France and Germany had opposed the war, but jumped on the imperial chariot after the fall of Baghdad, saying that the war was wrong but they could not oppose the occupation! Democracy has become truncated and hollowed-out by neoliberal economics. All over the world, with the exception of Cuba and Venezuela, neoliberal norms are in place. Gangster capitalism does not require democracy. It can even become a burden.

*In your autobiography entitled* Street-Fighting Years, *re-released in 2005 in extended form,*[3] *you analyze, among other things, the anti-Vietnam protest movement in the 1960s. What would you consider the most striking differences between the 1960s and today, especially when it comes to the conditions for political dissidence, or a peace movement that could be instrumental in ending a war that is killing thousands of civilians?*

The movements that arose during the 1960s of the last century were situated in an epoch of wars, decolonization and revolutions. Utopia seemed possible. Today, capitalism has turned the world upside down. This does not mean nothing can be achieved. Latin America shows the opposite, and the conditions for dissidence are still there, but there is a continuing discussion on agency: which social force will achieve change? It's an open question. It will be answered in its own time. Meanwhile the struggle continues.

*A popular Leftist slogan of the last couple of years has been to "change the world without taking power," or in other words, to stage colorful, polymorphous guerrilla-like events in the streets without ever pursuing dissent or protest in institutionalized forms. Do you see any positive prospects for strategies like that?*

No. I have never liked that slogan. It was born out of despair and defeats, but was always stupid. The Bolivarian process in Venezuela has made the slogan laughable.

## Violence, Seen and Unseen

*In dealing with the developments leading to the current occupation scenario, as well as Western societies haunted by fears of "fundamentalist terrorists," one of your arguments concerns the relationship of "visible" to "invisible violence." To put it simply, a kind of structural, global-economic violence on the part of the West has been counteracted by a few spectacular visible acts that have gained an immense degree of media attention. What role do particular kinds of fundamentalisms actually play on both sides of this divide—in contradistinction, for instance, to the view of a generalized "clash of civilizations"?*

My argument is not so much related to "invisible violence." I think the causes of 9/11 and the attacks on Madrid and London are directly related to Western occupation of Muslim lands. Here I agree with the work on this subject being done at the University of Chicago: Robert Pape's admirable analysis *Dying to Win: The Strategic Logic of Suicide Terrorism* (2005).[4] Pape denies strongly that Islamic ultra-fundamentalism is the root cause of terrorism. He argues that, "The central fact is that overwhelmingly suicide-terrorist attacks are not driven by religion as much as they are by a clear strategic objective: to compel modern democracies to withdraw military forces from the territory that the terrorists view as their homeland. From Lebanon to Sri Lanka to Chechnya to Kashmir to the West Bank, every major suicide-terrorist campaign—over 95 percent of all the incidents—has had as its central objective to compel a democratic state to withdraw ... Since suicide terrorism is mainly a response to foreign occupation and not Islamic fundamentalism, the use of heavy military force to transform Muslim societies over there, if you would, is only likely to increase the number of suicide terrorists coming at us."[5]

*The London bombings last July were carried out by second-generation immigrants (who are officially not immigrants but British citizens). The threat, so to speak, does not come from "outside," nor is it effected by a "foreign (evil) force," but now takes its point of departure from within society. Is the picture of terrorist acts aimed at "Western civilization" somehow changing with events like these?*

In my new book *Rough Music*[6] I discuss this question at length. I think it is now widely accepted in Britain that the July 7 attacks were a response to Britain's involvement in the Iraq war. Attempts by Blair and his embedded journalists to deny this have backfired.

*The so-called "war on terror" seems to have engendered some of the very evils that the "coalition of the willing" set out to fight against in the very first place. Concerning the situation in Iraq, a popular argument nowadays goes that there is no way back now, or in other words, that the occupation forces cannot be withdrawn without an even greater catastrophe resulting from this. What would an alternative route to democratization (of Iraq and other Arab states) look like—one that does not rely on a brutally enforced "liberation"?*

The situation in Iraq is awful. There is now a near-universal agreement that the Western occupation of Iraq has turned out to be an unmitigated disaster, first for the people of Iraq themselves, and secondly for the Western soldiers sent by scoundrel politicians to die in a foreign land. The grammar of deceit utilized by Bush, Blair and sundry neocon/neolib apologists to justify the war has lost all credibility. Despite the embedded journalists and the non-stop propaganda, the bloody images refuse to go away. A savage chaos disfigures the country. On the fringes of the occupying armies, rival militias vie for control. Water and electricity are still sporadically supplied. The hospitals and schools barely function. Iraq under Anglo-Saxon occupation is in a worse state than it was during the previous decade under the sanctions imposed by the West and implemented by the United Nations. The sooner the occupying armies leave, the better.

*The US-led war on terror has also led to particularly striking developments in the realm of human rights, both in the homeland and abroad, where not only the events at Guantanamo or Abu Ghraib stand out, but policies like the so-called "extraordinary rendition program,"*[7] *through which terror suspects can be delivered to countries where torture is performed on them (something that US authorities are not allowed to do in the homeland and that they officially deny). Can you comment on this development?*

Torture is nothing new in the history of 20th-century empires. The only reason to be surprised is because of the propaganda assault by the West, which has stressed "human rights." Harold Pinter put it very well in his Nobel Prize acceptance speech: "It never happened. Nothing ever happened. Even while it was happening it wasn't happening. It didn't matter. It was of no interest. The crimes of the United States have been systematic, constant, vicious, remorseless, but very few people have actually talked about them. You have to hand it to America. It has exercised a quite clinical manipulation of power worldwide while masquerading as a force for universal good. It's a brilliant, even witty, highly successful act of hypnosis."[8]

*Coming back to the issue of amnesia, a particular case in question seems to be the aftermath of recent natural disasters. While the hurricane scenarios in the southern USA gained almost undisrupted media attention, an event like the earthquake in northern Pakistan seemed to be gone from public perception after something like two days. In what ways could one speak of "second and third-class victims," or of a "media racism" when it comes to the victims of natural catastrophes?*

It's always the same. In Pakistan, no Westerners were involved or died. The media vultures descend on tragedy, pick the entrails of the dead and wounded with their cameras and then depart. Meanwhile Cuba has sent over a thousand doctors in the remotest regions of the country and has set up three camp hospitals and is distributing free medicines.

[1] Cf. www.iraqbodycount.org and http://antiwar.com
[2] Tariq Ali, "Tortured Civilizations: Islam and the West," in *The Walrus*, September 2004, p. 52–61 (www.walrusmagazine.com).
[3] Tariq Ali, *Street-Fighting Years: An Autobiography of the Sixties.* London/New York: Verso 2005.
[4] Robert A. Pape, *Dying to Win: The Strategic Logic of Suicide Terrorism.* New York: Random House 2005.
[5] "The Logic of Suicide Terrorism: Interview with Robert A. Pape," in *The American Conservative*, July 18, 2005 (www.amconmag.com/2005_07_18/article.html).
[6] Tariq Ali, *Rough Music: Blair/Bombs/Baghdad/London/Terror.* London/New York: Verso 2005.
[7] Cf. Jane Mayer, "Outsourcing Terror. The battle over 'extraordinary rendition'," in *The New Yorker*, February 14 & 21, 2005, p. 106–123.
[8] http://nobelprize.org/literature/laureates/2005/pinter-lecture-g.html.

# *Terror Weather*
# Conversation with Bill Ayers

Interview conducted in November 2001.

On September 11, 2001, an article with the title "No Regrets for a Love of Explosives" appeared in the *New York Times.** Bill Ayers, once wanted by the FBI and now working as a university professor, had just published his memoirs, *Fugitive Days*,** something that caused a furor all over the USA. As a key member of the activist movement "Weather Underground," which started up in 1969, Ayers took part in many symbolic acts of violence in the early 1970s directed against military and government institutions. As a result, he ended up on the FBI's wanted list, along with many other members of the organization.

Among the prominent targets of actions carried out by "Weather" were the Capitol, the headquarters of the National Guard, and, in 1972, the Pentagon.*** Nobody was ever hurt except in one explosion in New York that claimed the lives of three "Weather" members, including Ayers' then girlfriend, Diana Oughton. Since then, the "Weather" mythos has provided material for a large number of artistic reappraisals, the most prominent of these probably being Emile de Antonio's film *Underground* (1974) and Raymond Pettibon's video *Weathermen '69: The Whole World Is Watching* (1989). From about 1980 on, the former members finally began to emerge from the underground. Some of them were arrested or gave themselves up to the authorities, which often had no consequences for them, as many of the legal proceedings had to be called off on account of the illegal methods used in FBI investigations.

When the feature article appeared in the *New York Times* on September 11, no one could know what significance the episode on "bombing the Pentagon" recounted by Bill Ayers would suddenly acquire on this very day; indeed, what sort of re-encoding the concept of terror would altogether undergo in the USA. All at once, the question arose of how opposition to the worldwide imperialism of the USA—which has perhaps only taken on other forms since the time of the Vietnam War—and to a US-dominated process of globalization was able to keep going. What changes do critics of official US politics find in the scenario since then, and what criteria will have to guide this criticism in future? Bill Ayers runs through historic phases of symbolic politics of resistance, and explains the facets of a new, old conclusion: "New Morning—Changing Weather."

* Dinitia Smith, "No Regrets for a Love of Explosives: In a Memoir of Sorts, a War Protestor Talks of Life With the Weathermen," *The New York Times*, September 11, 2001, p. E1, E3.

** Bill Ayers, *Fugitive Days: A Memoir.* Boston: Beacon Press 2001.

*** The history of the Weather Underground is well documented in Ron Jacob, *The Way the Wind Blew: A History of the Weather Underground.* London, New York: Verso 1997.

CH *The current "War on Terror" brings to mind a historical period in the US—the late 1960s and early 1970s—in which there still seemed to be a political option that was conceived the other way round: precisely targeted acts of violence (in which you yourself participated), termed "terror" by the State, in order to end a war that was getting totally out of control and could not be justified by any means. What are your feelings vis-à-vis this historical "reversal," these suddenly changed roles?*

BA I'm not sure "historical reversal" is the term—deception, imprecision, and perversion come to mind, but this is all purely rhetorical. From 1965–1975 the US government waged an illegal and immoral war—a war of terror—against the country and the people of Vietnam. Whole regions of Vietnam were designated "free-fire zones" by the US, cities were bombed indiscriminately, civilians were murdered by the tens of thousands, and this was not mere "collateral damage," the perverse

Pentagon term of art for mayhem and murder, but deliberate, cold-eyed policy. In 1965 I was arrested in a non-violent protest inside a draft board—a relatively small outcry practically drowned out at the time by a considerably larger pro-war counter-demonstration. For the next years, I organized, I spoke up, I wrote, and I demonstrated against murderous US policy, and I was arrested in escalating acts of militant opposition to terror. By 1968 the overwhelming majority of Americans had been won to oppose the war, but the war continued and escalated—we didn't know it then, of course, but after President Johnson was driven from office, the war would unwind for another seven years and over a million-and-a-half more human beings would be sacrificed in the American-built death chamber in Southeast Asia.

Those of us who opposed the war searched desperately for what more we could do to end it—some joined the Democratic Party and attempted to build a Left within it, others went to work in factories and tried to organize the industrial working class, others moved on in their professional lives, and a small group of us—young, determined, somewhat despairing in that time—decided to build a clandestine capacity to survive what we thought was an escalating oppression at home, and simultaneously a capacity for illegal and armed resistance to the war and racism. In my book I describe a moment when a few of us flirted with the idea of matching official terror with a terror of our own, but we never did. We pulled back, and in fact, never killed or even injured anyone. We defended our actions as extreme measures employed in the face of an international emergency. In that sense—and in light of the fact that every day the war dragged on a couple of thousand more human beings were murdered—we were entirely restrained.

*One of the guiding slogans of the movement you participated in was "Bring the War Home!": let the war-makers of the military-industrial complex get a feel of what they are inflicting on innocent civilians thousands of miles away. Would you ever have imagined in your wildest dreams that this slogan could foreshadow something like the September 11 events?*

The events of September 11—a massive crime against humanity carried out, apparently, in the service of a monstrous reactionary ideology—were way beyond my imagination, far beyond anything anyone I've spoken to could have dreamed in their most heated nightmares. Turning commercial airliners into giant guided missiles controlled by highly skilled suicide bombers—the planning, the patience, the practice—it's all finally too much.

For decades I've challenged my students and other audiences to wonder with me how long the US—something like 5% of the world's population—could go merrily along in its determined innocence, its self-induced blindness, controlling and consuming the vast majority of the planet's wealth. Two billion of the world's six billion people lack the basics to survive; this winter millions of Afghans may well perish from starvation; and some of us routinely practice a habitual and extravagantly wasteful consumption, while a growing number of people can't consume enough to live another day. How high will we have to build the walls around ourselves to maintain that injustice? How deep the moats? How many of the barbarians at the gates will we be willing to slaughter to defend that imbalance? The arrogant self-designation, "the world's only superpower," sounds hollow and false following September 11.

*In your memoir,* Fugitive Days, *you write: "Everything was absolutely ideal on the day I bombed the Pentagon. The sky was blue. The birds were singing. And the bastards were finally going to get what was coming to them." How do you feel about this passage after the recent events? On the last pages of your book, you seem to be somewhat ambivalent about the use of bombings as a means to increase global justice.*

I re-read *Fugitive Days* after September 11, and on occasion had to stop in order to catch my breath or wipe my eyes. The opening of the chapter on bombing the Pentagon was one such occasion. As a writer I decided to enter that difficult, complex territory with a chirpy, light-hearted tone, to work the style, that is, against the content. After September 11 nothing much felt light-hearted, certainly not the phrase "bomb the Pentagon" with the image of a commercial airliner transformed into a bomb which would randomly incinerate hundreds of innocent people. But that chapter does something else—it narrates the stories of two groups of young Americans. One group, determined, somewhat despairing, a bit off the tracks, steels itself in order to put a small bomb in a pipe in the Pentagon in order to sound a searing alarm against the war. The act was designed as a symbol, and as intended, no one was hurt or injured. Another group of young Americans, frightened, despairing, and also off the tracks, enters a Vietnamese village and kills 347 people outright, and then rapes, loots, maims, tortures, burns homes, and slaughters animals. The intention was partly symbolic, a symbol of random death and ongoing danger, and it was harrowingly real as well. The question that I raise in the chapter is this: what is terrorism?

I wrote a memoir, not a manifesto nor a polemic nor a diatribe nor a defense. I try to capture something of the resonant feeling of those times, the color and the texture and the tone, and to tell the story of how one boy lived his life, negotiated the tricky terrain of chance and choice, woke up to a world in flames, and came of age inside a whirlwind of violence.

Of course, one of the terrible facts of our world is the existence of violence—not as the tactical choice of a few, but as the core characteristic of a wide range of social relations. In our own history the existence of slavery is the clearest example—whole generations could grow up and die and never lift a hand against one another and yet the relationship, if adequately examined and understood, was violent at its very core. Colonialism is another such relationship. During the war against Vietnam every American was implicated in acts of violence—we knew what was being done in our names, we saw and read about instances of the terror in gory detail, and we were called upon to watch and to accede. Many of us resisted, some of us took extreme measures.

I don't believe, however, that tactics should ever elevate above strategy or principle. Global justice doesn't grow out of the barrel of a gun nor is it at the end of a lighted fuse. Justice will come from the hearts and minds of millions of people hoping for a fairer and more peaceful world, and stirred to act together against the obstacles to their liberation. The measure, then, of the value of any tactic is how it serves the goal of educating or organizing many, many other people. This doesn't rule out militant, or extreme, or creative, or even armed action—it simply offers a standard from which to judge.

*In retrospect, do you think the campaign you started under the name Weather Underground did contribute to the end of the Vietnam War? If so, in what respect?*

I do. We were a small part of the largest international anti-war movement in history. The anti-war movement limited the options of the war-makers, allowing a range of progressive options and movements to emerge and flourish. The Vietnamese people themselves, of course, mobilized and united, were the decisive element and force in their own national liberation.

## Dissent and Violence

*The Weather campaign strictly targeted military institutions, and institutions alone, not the people representing them, or people working there in possibly low-paid jobs. The president back then, Richard Nixon, called the actions "the work of cowardly terrorists." What is your reaction when you hear exactly the same words under today's circumstances?*

While Richard Nixon had it wrong on both counts—we were neither cowardly nor terrorists—George Bush has it half wrong. Others have noted that you can call the September 11 bombers many things, but cowardly isn't one of them—they guided those planes right where they wanted them and went to their deaths in the process. They killed thousands of innocent people and they committed a massive crime against humanity, and, yes, they were terrorists. But the language—the catch-all labels and the easy, oft-repeated phrases—is imprecise and unhelpful as well. After all, a couple of decades ago, the US had the bright idea of arming these thugs (a gesture roundly condemned by the Left), calling them "freedom fighters" and aiming them at the Soviet Union. We called them right-wing fundamentalist zealots then, and that is a more accurate identifier today.

*Shortly before September 11, a young demonstrator was shot to death in Genoa by the Italian police at an anti-globalization rally. Again, this resonates with scenes from American history: after the incidents at Kent State and Jackson State University in 1970, when authorities fired into the crowds of demonstrators, killing and wounding lots of people, the president blamed it all on the victims ("when dissent turns to violence, it invites tragedy," he said). After Genoa, we heard exactly the same phrases. How far, do you think, have we actually progressed or moved from that scenario of 1970?*

I don't think we can quantify progress or motion so easily. The rulers will always blame the victims, of course, and they will forever turn a blind eye to even the most reasonable aspirations if they feel their power or their wealth threatened in the least. The issues that we faced thirty years ago—imperialism, racism, the growing disparity between rich and poor—challenge us today in new forms. Imperialism never means its withdrawals, and power concedes nothing without a demand. Every generation and every individual must find ways to name the obstacles to democracy and freedom concretely, and to move against them.

*What is your feel vis-à-vis the so called "anti-globalization movement"? Was it, in your opinion, on the right track to effectively challenge the new empire before September 11? Have their goals been discredited after the attacks?*

I take great heart and hope from the recent actions in Seattle, Washington, and Genoa. Young people woke up millions and began to forge an exciting new movement for social justice on a global scale. Recent events affirm the need to strengthen and extend the international movements for economic justice, environmental sanity, human rights and women's rights, and criminal justice.

*One of the first actions Weather undertook in 1969 was the blowing-up of a police statue at Haymarket Square in Chicago (opening the historic "Days of Rage"[1]). After the statue was re-erected again a year later, you blew it up a second time. The actions appear to have been motivated by a significant sense of humor?*

True—a kind of bratty, outrageous, juvenile delinquent sense of humor always rode along in the sidecar of our earnest self-righteousness.

*A lot of references of your movement came, of course, from pop culture. For instance, a lot of Bob Dylan was used: the line "You don't need a weather man to know which way the wind blows" gave the movement its initial name, his album title* New Morning *headed a communiqué in 1970, "Maggie's Farm" signified the Pentagon in your coded language. How important was that symbolic dimension of the "popular"?*

The youth culture was a culture of opposition—long hair, drugs, rock 'n' roll signified a resistant stance in the world. Of course, it was seized, sanitized, and commodified. Even in the 1960s, "THE SIXTIES" was being sold back to us as a product, bell-bottom pants, say, or revolutionary deodorant. Now, in the fog of nostalgia, it's worse—"The 1960s, Inc.," with an established group of scholars and commentators who attack all renegade accounts of the significance of that time and who defend their authorized views, their patents, through pieces in the *New York Times*. Janis Joplin's image is employed as a pitch-man for Mercedes Benz, John Lennon's for Apple, and Martin Luther King's, for chrissake, for everything. But culture was and is—as always—deeply contested territory.

*Your acts were primarily conceived as acts of "agitation" and "education" (as you write), mostly with respect to the racist circumstances in large parts of the US back then, and of course the attempted destruction of a people that a famous politician (or general?) wanted to see "bombed back to the Stone Age." In the light of the developments over the past two decades—how do you assess the success of these education endeavors, especially as regards the goal of making Americans face global political realities?*

On page 285 of *Fugitive Days* I write: "I think back to my childhood, to the houses in trim rows and the identical lawns and the neat fences; I remember everyone sleeping the deep American sleep, the sleep that still engulfs us and from which I worry we might not awake in time. We are living our isolated lives in our shattered communities, and in our names the US project shatters community everywhere—in the Middle East, in Colombia, in the Philippines. The world roils in agony and despair, the catastrophe deepens, and our ears are covered, our eyes are closed. Perhaps only the bark of bombs at our doors will shake us up after all." That paragraph startled and saddened me when I re-read it. It didn't have to happen. It shouldn't have happened. The people of America must wake up and insist that our country become a nation among nations, not a superpower or a superior state, but one among many.

## Authorized Amnesia

*In your memoir you also state—referring to the very problem of memory itself—that "America's foundational myths—are authorized amnesia." In a very illuminating passage you describe how the US is driven by a pragmatic sense of "Forget about it. Let's move on." Do you see this deeply entrenched ideology somehow change under present circumstances?*

I hope this period, so full of anguish, fear, and uncertainty, can become the occasion for fundamental change, for a new enlightenment, a reaching out. But, of course, the dogs of war are unleashed, the single-minded slogans are being chanted, and a suffocating unanimity is heard throughout America. I believe that while that unanimity is five miles wide, it is only a millimeter deep, and it must be resisted. Of course, all identity is forged through experience and built on memory, and that's as true for a national or social identity as for an individual one. This means that half-remembered events and false memories create a deformed identity capable of ever-repeating disasters. It's in the interest of the rich and the powerful to quash memory, and of the rest of us to fight for it, to invite debate, conflict, resolution, forgiveness, imagination, and truth.

*Currently, it appears that the traumas of September 11 have been totally handed over to two major disciplinary machines: to psychological counseling on the individual level, and to a patriotic war machine on the international, global level. There seems to be no intermediary ground in between these two apparatuses to deal with the crisis, to deal with it maybe on a reflective, socio-political level. Maybe you can comment on this?*

True, but this too is part of the territory we must engage and contest. When President Bush says, "Everything changed on September 11," we must respond that some things changed, but much remains the same, and that our dreams of justice and simple fairness are more intense than ever. We must resist this becoming the occasion for a massive transfer of wealth from public to private hands, for example, or the scuttling of civil liberties, actions already underway. When President Bush says, "Watch what you say," we should speak up with force and confidence, seek the truth, search our souls, and act on our contingent understandings as best we can. When President Bush repeats, "You're either with us or you're with the terrorists," we should respond, none of the above.

*Fugitive Days* gives a vivid account of life in the underground, presenting it in fine-grained everyday detail, without ever glorifying it. Would you say that individual memory usually tends more toward a glorification, or rather to a "neutralization" of traumatic pasts?*

It does both—but politically what's important is to tell the truth to power and to challenge "official memory," which is always anesthetizing and glorifying.

*The memoir ends when you and Bernardine Dohrn turned yourself over to the FBI in 1980. One wonders—and would have loved to read—what happened then, especially until you became Distinguished Professor of Education at the University of Chicago.*

See the sequel—perhaps I'll call it *Fugitive Nights.*

*Having been on the FBI's most-wanted poster (your wife, Bernardine Dohrn, was even once designated "the most dangerous woman in America" by J. Edgar Hoover), your life circumstances seem significantly changed since the Fugitive Days of the 1970s. Have you come to peace with America over those 20 years?*

I learned long ago, in fact it was a lesson taught to me by the Vietnamese, to make a distinction between the American people, indeed the American landscape and the American ideal, and the US government. I've tried for decades—even in the darkest, most despairing days—to find some balance between loving my life, participating whole-heartedly in the daily joys and challenges it brings—raising our children, teaching my students, taking long eclectic walks through the city at night—and at the same time being wide-awake, engaged in the society and the world, and willing to participate fully in what the known demands of me, to throw my fate on history's great wheel. So, no, I'm not at peace with the United States government and I probably never will be, but I am at peace with myself, with my family, and I experience the day-to-day life of an ordinary person living in happy opposition in extraordinary times.

[1] From October 8 to October 12, 1969, there were—sometimes escalating—protest actions in Chicago against the Vietnam War, the first demonstration of any real size planned by the Weathermen. The protest was also directed against legal proceedings then being taken against eight supposed "conspirators" (among them Jerry Rubin, Abbie Hoffman, Tom Hayden and Bobbie Seale), who one year before had organized demonstrations against the Democratic party convention in Chicago.

# *Tilting Effects, Disturbances*
# Conversation with Jean-Pierre Gorin

Interview conducted in October 2004.

Political cinema is among the oldest media in the history of moving pictures. However, it has always been a moot point what form politically effective films should take if they are to be more than Hollywood films with a different content. Right up until the present day, there has been a constant stream of new attempts to define political film, to conceive of a type of cinema going beyond the illusionary. One of these endeavours, going back to the late 1960s, was greatly influenced by the film-maker and theorist Jean-Pierre Gorin.

As a 25-year-old, Jean-Pierre Gorin approached the then star director of the Nouvelle Vague, Jean-Luc Godard, to found with him the group Dziga Vertov in 1968. In the course of their many years of collaboration, they made a number of low-budget movies, which Gorin nowadays likes to call "garage films" or "punk movies." In 1972 this form of fast, improvisatory political film activity slowly came to an end. Gorin went to the United States, where he continued to work on experimental documentary films, as well as taking up a teaching post at the University of California in San Diego where he is still exploring the political dimensions of cinema.

CH *At the time when you first became involved in filmmaking, one of the main principles—and you were actually a co-author of this—was no longer to make political films, but to make films political. How would you go about elaborating this distinction in retrospect?*

J-PG In the late 1960s, there was a need to define the possibility of a type of political cinema that was not locked in the idea of agitprop. Or what had happened to the idea of agitprop, which of course was greatly influenced by the Stalinist experience and Social Realism. We were a group of people who thought there was a legacy that nobody really wanted to talk about—partly through laziness, partly because of a reactionary desire to define once and for all what cinema was, and what it was supposed to be doing. So a first decision was—and this actually came from me, not from Godard—to make an explicit reference to Dziga Vertov, whom very few people still knew at the time.

What was so extraordinary about Vertov was that, in the early years of the Russian revolution, he was the first one to theorize, or hint at, what we now know as the idea of media. The idea that there was something that existed beyond film, that there was something coming to the fore which would be called media. That film, which had almost imperially ruled the highs and lows of culture, was—like all empires—coming to an end. And that this would have consequences which one should not necessarily lament. We thought that cinema, by rethinking itself along this Vertovian idea of media, might be able to reinvent itself. And one place where this reinvention seemed likely to happen was precisely political cinema. This is one way to look at the context retrospectively, but I am not quite sure if we saw things quite so uniquely at the time.

*There was also a certain polemics directed against a particular type of political cinema, wasn't there?*

Yes, definitely. You have to remember that we were not so much talking to the public in general. We were more interested in talking politically, especially to people on the Left. And we were quite struck by the fact that, for quite a while, the Left had been aesthetically as reactionary as it gets. I think that some of the radicality of the films done by the Dziga Vertov group derived precisely from the fact that they did not care and weren't afraid to put themselves out on a limb. At the time, a lot of people interpreted the phrase "to make film political" as a proclamation of collective creation. But that was not really a delusion we had. In the Dziga Vertov group, we were essentially two people, and we were not fooling anybody about that. Although there were other people gravitating toward us, we were very plain about the fact that this was essentially an enterprise generated between Godard and myself.

What we meant went well beyond the idea that collective creation would bring salvation. Rather, we thought that there was a need to reflect on the history of representation, on what political cinema had been. What ruled at the time was mostly realistic representation, and what people called "political film" was primarily film in which the figures were involved in some political activities, but apart from that remained pretty much within the formal tropes of classical Hollywood cinema. Thus, the question was constantly put in terms of distribution:

film was supposed to be political because it would reach the greatest possible audience. We thought that all these self-evident truths were maybe not so self-evident, that they were banalities that had been repeated time and again, but had not changed anything. It was not very interesting to keep thinking that the only way to make political statements was films like *The Battle Of Algiers* (1966) or *Z* (1968).

*The films of the Dziga Vertov group attempted a kind of re-invention of cinema and wanted to install a kind of counter-cinema. At the same time, the films were widely appropriative, borrowing from genres like the Western in* Vent d'est *(1969), or using a kind of television-report style in* Lotte in Italia *(1969) and even forms like the courtroom drama in* Vladimir et Rosa *(1971). They experimented with a radical newness of cinema, while at the same time ripping off all sorts of materials.*

This is exactly what it was—and very consciously so. One way to make films political was, for us, to always be aware of the conditions of production as well as the conditions of distribution. A lot of those films were produced with money from television—and supposedly distributed through TV. They were in a way taking on this institution, being very conscious of the kind of flow of visual and audio information that is organized by TV. The question was how to create a glitch in that flow. How to produce something that, for an hour or 96 minutes, could create a moment of formal disruption. We were very aware of the fact that this moment could only be created as a formal distortion. This implied two things: that in some way you had to recall forms that were commonly used in the medium itself; and that you had to transform them. The political aspect lay exactly in this kind of switcher effect.

For instance, at the end of *Lotte in Italia*, a TV anchorperson talks for four minutes, but very differently from the usual television style. Before that, the film is about images separated by long periods of black—which is already a major interruption of the flow of images on TV and which gets filled in by different types of information. We were interested in the fact that, among other things, film called upon tropes and forms that existed in the present as tactics, but that it also called upon experiences that were highly interior. In that respect, *Lotte in Italia* is like a repetition of the Kuleshov experiment. Something that people did not want to hear at the time was that you do not decide to be radical, but that you have to work on your radicality. And working on your radicality had very much to do with a certain kind of knowledge, an examination and resurrection of the past.

At that time, Pasolini did a film for UNESCO which he shot in Yemen, and which ends with the phrase "never underestimate the revolutionary strength of the past." A lot of the films that we did cannot be understood—and they were not at all understood at the time—if you do not see that they function like a bridge. *Vent d'est*, for instance, is anchored in certain things that Griffith did, as well in a certain tradition of agitation theatre. In some ways, its radicality is the reproduction and reactivating of that tradition. So it should be no surprise that all kinds of pre-existing modes were appropriated, called into question, displaced—like the genre of the Western, which was an allusion to the fact that a lot of left-wing militants loved spaghetti Westerns. *Lotte in Italia*, by comparison, is typically a television film, and *Vladimir et Rosa*, which to my mind has aged extremely well, is a kind of saturated soundtrack that in its strident way draws on the best of pop and, in some respects, anticipates hip-hop. Seeing these films 30 years after they were made still gives you the impression that they were very much "Alive," with a capital A. If critics had been serious about them, and if you think of what was held up as the grand examples of truly interesting political art at the time, we would have come out as geniuses!

*Were the films generally trashed at the time?*

Generally, yes. But the critics who trashed them did not understand what was going on. And the ones who said great things about them did not understand either. Mostly, people were baffled by the fact that Jean-Luc could be involved in such stuff, so they completely dismissed him. When they were excited they could not take on the fact that the films had actually been made by two people.

*Coming back again to the notion of making films political: you make it clear that the politics of a film have to pass through its form, and do not have that much to do with content, plot and so on. This is especially true of the early Dziga Vertov group films from 1969 to 1971. By comparison,* Tout va bien, *made in 1972, seems to put a lot more emphasis on plot and its two big stars (Jane Fonda and Yves Montand). How did that development come about?*

Well, we knew that we could not keep going materially. Around 1971, we were facing a number of problems. For instance, we noticed that the kind of social energy that had given rise to the Dziga Vertov group was disappearing. Also, the mode of production was getting more and more difficult and restrained. *Tout va bien* translates all that—for instance, to continue a desire that would otherwise not continue, hoping that we could export these things into a larger context. In the end—and there was really some fundamental honesty about it—it really expresses, like no other film at the time, that something was receding and ending. It does not endorse the discourse of "gauchisme," but it registers a kind of machine in which a complexity of voices gets heard, and it also tries to confront the contradictions of a certain practice. Within all that, it also has a very personal tone—which I think is not perceptible to a lot of people. After that, we did *Letter to Jane* (1972), which is still an amazing film and which sums up a lot of questions. The whole development from *Vent d'est* to *Letter to Jane*, not forgetting films like *British Sounds* or *Pravda*, was an extremely rich experience.

## Aspects of a Cultural Revolution

*Something extremely important in these films is the emphasis on sound in relation to the image. As you say, the project that Godard had started earlier very much consisted in freeing cinema from the tyranny of the literary model and bringing to the fore a "cinema of sound" while also opening up cinema toward painting. Which of these directions had priority?*

What Godard did—and of course, he was not the only one, but he did it in the most explicit fashion—was to start with the idea that there was a certain dominance of the literary model in cinema. So he said, ok, let's accept that dominance—but it does not have to be Balzac or Dickens. I still remember a panel on which Henri-Georges Clouzot said that a film should have a beginning, a middle, and an end; and

Jean-Luc replied, "I totally agree, but not necessarily in that order." To me, this seemed like a brilliant way to define the problem. Once you apply different types of literary models, and this phrase sums this up quite clearly, film is pushed in a different direction, one that has nothing to do with literature, but everything to do with painting. Once the scene becomes more autonomous, all the plastic properties of the scene become more important. If you look at Godard's films you will see that he practically invented visual arts movies, and that he did them by the tone. Of course, this soon became the rule of the game, while less and less interesting results were produced.

In the late 1960, it became obvious that the luxuriousness and painterliness of the image was increasingly employed by people who thought that, if it looked like a painting, that was already enough. By contrast, Godard was not really interested in making the image look like a painting, but in making it function like a painting. At the moment when I intervened (around 1968), the dependence of film on painterliness was, at the one end, starting to evolve into the ridiculous, the imitation of painters and so on; but, at the other, it was really starting to catch up with its model, with what painting was preoccupied with at the time, properties like flatness and so on. That was really what we did: devaluate the literary model, make the image as "unjuicy" as possible and really work the whole film from the sound end. Of course, the results still looked very painterly. There is absolutely no doubt that *Vent d'est* and *Vladimir et Rosa* are gorgeous looking films, even if that's "gorgeous-shitty." One way to achieve this was to create these bizarre soundtracks that use the kind of saturation of speech and discourse that existed at the time, but really focus on the layering. At the end of that period, there is an emergence of the soundtrack, a new possibility for the musicality of the soundtrack. It is not there yet, but in a way it feels like the end of the talkies. The sheer saturation starts to jam your ears.

*The relation of film to sound and painting has a lot to do with the opening up of film toward media. In more recent years, this has come true in a very different sense: that is to say, the opening up toward the whole audio-visual realm that surrounds us these days, sometimes in very obnoxious ways. Back at that time, TV could in fact serve as a kind of model, for instance in* Lotte in Italia. *What hopes were actually connected to the institution of television? Did this primarily have an instrumental aspect, of maybe reaching a wider audience? Or was there something in the medium itself that was promising?*

I think both. The crass, practical aspect of it was that these films could only be financed within the medium of television. Also, there was a kind of left-wing liberal bureaucracy within the space of television. TV was of course a Moloch—it functioned like a huge common grid that had an enormous appetite for images and sounds. Within that, even people like us could find a possibility of functioning. The other aspect was that it seemed to be a terrain of political intervention, no matter how late something was broadcast—in the case of our films, usually at two in the morning. But there is also a historical dimension to this, related to the whole history of cinema. For Lumière, filming was not just showing workers coming out of the factory, but also filming a baby's breakfast. This was a gesture of considerable importance: namely, that the private could be spectacularized by the very people involved in it. Suddenly, everybody could make an image of her- or himself. In fact, Kodak derived far more of its revenue from this spectacularization of the private than it did from Hollywood. Cinema dealt with this notion of the private and sent it into another realm.

But there was still another side to this, and Jean-Luc defined it quite well when he said that cinema took us away from mummy and daddy and sent us out on the streets; and that was so dangerous that they had to invent television. In TV, there is a tendency to channel the source and flow of images back into the private, where the conditions of viewing are radically different from those in a theatre. But that also opened up a kind of political space, because films could be made that, in a random and uncontrollable way, would be a kind of looped intervention; films that grabbed people as they were set in their familiar environments and showed them these bizarre things on the screen. So for us, this provided a very interesting terrain to intervene. We did not know exactly the effects this would have, but we were persuaded that people would stay in front of the screen because of what we did and what we were. Without our work, someone like Alan Clarke, who made *Elephant* (1989), could not have used the medium of television in the way he did. I am not saying that we were the originators, but we were definitely part of a movement in which such questions were raised.

*When did it become clear that the cultural revolution was not going to be effected through television?*

Very early on. But the problem was not so much making it a vector for the cultural revolution. It was more a question of creating glitches in the system. This is something that we were constantly faulted for. But people really made us more naïve than we actually were, and it served them quite well because they did not see the questions we were asking. I am not saying we were absolutely right—we had plenty of naïve hopes, and the films were in some respects complicated, rhetorical and strident. But we were also something else—which is the more interesting part of it.

*You often talk about the films of the Dziga Vertov group as being "garage films" or "punk films."* Vladimir et Rosa, *you said, could also be thought of as Johnny Rotten and Sid Vicious deciding to make a film. Punk, in its total assault on culture, always had a very nihilistic side to it, whereas you constantly stress the element of hope in connection with your films. Can you elaborate on this contradiction?*

For me, this is not a contradiction. I am interested in art that gives me hope. This does not necessarily mean the notion that something can be changed, but rather that something else can be done, that the way in which things are put together can be radically changed. If you are a filmmaker, you are not condemned to do what everybody else is doing. Also, it does not mean that you will necessarily fail just because you have fewer means. Whether in literature, music, or media, I have always been excited by work that opens up a terrain. Sometimes the work that gives you hope can be very nihilistic in nature. Critics have not yet grasped the big change that happened with Nietzsche when he objected to Kant by saying that the reference to categories outside the work, like the beautiful or the sublime, is a radical mind-fuck. Rather, art has to be anchored in the gesture of the maker and great works are promises of hope. Sometimes, you have promises of hope that function very differently than you would expect.

*Something I also want to ask concerns the relation of the Dziga Vertov group to the Maoism of the time, as well as to other groupings on the Left. In France, for instance, the cultural revolution was also propagated by groups like La Gauche prolétarienne, who put forward ideas of popular justice, or popular tribunals. From today's standpoint, this seems quite stunning, and even someone like André Glucksmann admits how close this actually was to left-wing terrorism, like the RAF in Germany. What was your relation to "La Gauche prolétarienne"?*

Well, there was a sense in 1968 that the people who had always ruled the roost were still ruling the roost, and would end up ruling the roost. In order to understand this, you only have to read *The Demons* by Dostoevsky. This is the great novel about the absolute twilight and delirium that existed in pre- and post-revolutionary Russia, and that existed around 1968 as well. Glucksmann, who later on meditated on popular justice, was one of its great promoters. I never was. I always thought this was pretty hilarious and demented, but it was part of the big delirium. And why should it not be? It was the end of an enormous history that had left a lot of people on the ground; something that had started around 1917 and had gone through many avatars. All those groups took part in a larger historical enterprise in which, effectively, the ideology that had dominated Marxism and the 50 years prior to the 1960s became extinct. There was madness, but this was all linked to some giant psycho-drama that had existed way before.

*When do you think a rupture occurred with that kind of thinking? At the end of* Tout va bien, *for instance, there still seem to be highly charged and unresolved contradictions in the air. In the great last scene, shot in the supermarket, a little revolt starts, but it is not a full-blown revolution. It somehow gives you the sense that a revolution is yet to come.*

That was what was happening. At the same time, it was the glacial edge, and a certain activism had come to an end. The truth is—and every time I tell this story nobody wants to believe it—that we were not involved in politics. We were involved in the fact of making films. And that happened to be first and foremost a renewed reflection on an effective change in the ways film would be made, and the ways it would be perceived. This is not a denial of what was going on, but we were not party members. Nobody was a party member at that time, nobody had a carrying card. "La Gauche prolétarienne" was a fluctuant organization that had part of its headquarters at the Ecole normale supérieure in Paris. But it was also part of a "gauchiste" movement that left marks in many different places. Things were a lot more fluid than people would like to acknowledge today.

## Inside Is Outside

*Moving on to your "American period," in particular your migration to the US West Coast in 1975, I first wanted to ask if you found the same countercultural climate there as in Paris? Or was the situation totally different?*

In fact, it was. I did not go to the places where what I had done would have secured me a safe position, like New York, San Francisco or Chicago. Instead, I went to San Diego because I was interested in the work of Manny Farber. I did not go to the US because I thought I could find the remains of the counterculture there. I went to a place that happens to be the seventh largest city in the US but which is culturally very dead. Coming from the Dziga Vertov group, I was mostly asking myself questions about fiction, about how fiction was possible. I was concerned with the re-invention of fiction through a documentary perspective, which also had to do with the idea—entertained by the Dziga Vertov group—of information as drama. I started to do films that took on the experience of exile and migration, and created a genre that was about the idea of family, in the style of a fictional documentary.

This was something, once again, that people absolutely could not understand at the time. For instance, when I put out *Poto and Cabengo* (1979), it took seventeen years for French television to show it. But I was very conscious of what I was doing, and *Poto and Cabengo* was really pushing the idea of doing primarily sound films. It was very much about language, and the idea of layering, and it was about creating a type of narrative where you end up with a set of questions more than answers. After that, I did another film that was even more aggressively a machine of that type—*Routine Pleasures* (1986), which is a completely unclassifiable movie. And then there is the gangster film *My Crasy Life* (1991), which is the most classical of the three. So where does that leave me? At a place where I feel that it is time to reinvent something else. Which I think has to do with the image.

*The trajectory of the three films is very much about the gradual process of getting inside American culture; from the position of the complete outsider to someone who has achieved a certain closeness, even to the gangster milieu (the Samoans in* My Crasy Life*). Can you briefly recapitulate that move?*

The trilogy is about language, about the relationship to the Other. The three films re-trace an experience that is a fundamental experience in America: it is a place made by exiles, for exiles. It is actually very difficult to talk about exile in the US because it is so general, because everybody comes from somewhere else. *Poto and Cabengo*, for instance, goes back to comic strips and the idea that, in this kind of visual representation, you find a particular type of story that has existed among the Germans, Irish, Jewish and so on. Among them all, you find a desperate fight against the English language, a struggle with the idea of polyphony or poly-voicious recordings. At the second stage, after you have arrived and mastered the language, you ask yourself, "Am I inside?" That is what I wanted to do with *Routine Pleasures*. But this becomes a kind of fantasy, because the horizon always recedes. So to be inside is to be outside—which is part of the duality of the American experience. The third stage, then, is to be so inside that you can effectively perceive a type of language that is in fact a gangster language. That is why *My Crasy Life* is written with an "s." Also, the questions in the film are not asked by me, but by the gangsters themselves. It is about penetrating that kind of mystery.

*What made you first become a filmmaker was, as you said, seeing Straub/Huillet's* Not Reconciled. *Although you did not understand a word, it made you feel like you had learned a whole language through that film. Do you see any similarities between the condition back then and today's political climate, or for that matter, a new* Not Reconciled *somewhere on the horizon?*

I really think that the people I am producing are quite promising in that respect. For instance, I am producing *Zigzag*, the first film of Judy Jy Ah Min, a young Korean-American woman, which contains an enormous amount of energy. It takes on, in a very radical fashion, the aesthetic nature of the digital. Although it does not refer to the Straubs or others, there is a kind a re-invention taking place. Altogether, the people I am producing are more marked by music than they are by cinema. Not necessarily by popular music but by the musical idea of layering. They are also very fluent in computers and new media. They are very familiar with the existence of things as layers, or screens of information, and how to pass from one level to the next. Although I am not quite able to analyze or foresee what will come out of this, I see a kind of energy and push that is quite amazing.

# *Mutuality of the Moment*
# Conversation with Irit Rogoff

Interview conducted in September 2006.

Irit Rogoff's work spans quite a wide variety of subjects, ranging from postcolonial and feminist theory to issues of critical geography and migrant subjectivity. However, what has become most commonly associated with her name is the theoretical outline of "visual culture"—an umbrella term, whose content, as Rogoff herself explains, could be almost anything. The following conversation revolves around the possible contours of visual culture as well as one of its central agendas, viz. the problem of participation.

Rogoff trained as an art historian, but her position as the chair of Visual Culture at London's Goldsmiths College has led her more and more into the realm of non-academic work. Recently, she has been involved as a curator in two major exhibitions, one called *De-Regulation*,* a show about "how the work of Kutlug Ataman makes us do other things than what is usually associated with art." Another project titled *Academy*** was a compound of several projects that were situated at the intersections of museum, pedagogy and the establishment of new knowledge structures.

Rogoff's quest for "unhomed geographies" and an "active form of un-belonging" goes way beyond mere geographical or disciplinary matters. Rather, it can be considered a life-long project, or as she herself elaborates: "Though I am currently on my fourth country and third language, none of my displacements has been in the least tragic, unlike the plight of those forced to leave homelands for political and intellectual reasons. My movement has had to do with a restless curiosity, opportunities and the making of certain choices, not much more, and in the process I have acquired some skills in cross-cultural translations and in adapting to situations ... Though my movements do reflect, to some extent, the colonial beliefs in the scholastic and cultural superiority of Europe and the United States over those of my native Middle East, they are equally part of the professionalization and global circulation of the late twentieth-century world of ideas. Nevertheless my own displacement entails complex daily negotiations between all the cultures and languages and histories which inhabit me, resulting in the suspension of belief in the possibility of either coherent narratives or sign systems that can actually reflect straightforward relations between subjects, places and identities."***

* *De-Regulation – with the work of Kutlug Ataman* (2006/07), Museum van Hedendaagse Kunst, Antwerp, Belgium; Herzliya Museum of Art, Herzliya, Israel.

** *Academy. Learning from Art /Learning from the Museum* (2006), Van Abbemuseum, Eindhoven, Netherlands; Museum van Hedendaagse Kunst, Antwerp, Belgium.

*** Irit Rogoff, *Terra Infirma: Geography's Visual Culture*. London/New York: Routledge 2000, p. 5 f.

CH *Over the past couple of years, you have been at the forefront of theorizing "visual culture"—not just as a new object of study, but also as a new kind of methodological endeavor. What prompted this particular move beyond the theorization of the individual or isolated image that might also be dealt with in art historical or media-theoretic terms? What brought about this new configuration of visual culture that you also understand as a new "mode of knowledge"?*

IR I think I would answer that on several levels. Initially, I came out of art history, and I came out of a particularly narrow training in art history. Once I stopped being a student and started to become a more independent researcher, I was wasting huge amounts of time fighting with that discipline. I began every project by first outlining how art history would deal with this, and then finding some procedure that was the exact opposite. Around the mid-1990s—a time when we first got e-mail at university—

I started corresponding very intensively with Nick Mirzoeff, who was also working in the United States at that point. We kept thinking about how to develop an approach that would be a move sideways from art history, so that we could deal with particular issues without fighting the disciplinary fight. That, in a way, was the first move toward visual culture.

At the heart of this move, there was a problem that Derrida characterized very well when he said that boundaries are nothing more than the limits of the possible—no matter if they are narrow or expanded boundaries. I realized that if I stayed within a certain discipline, I would spend the rest of my life expanding its boundaries. But what I was really interested in was an unbounded sphere and the question of whether that was possible. The emphasis on the visual was accidental in a way: we came from art history, we had some kind of grounding in visual materials, an investment in something called art, and so it became visual culture. Of course, there is a big difference between fighting in every which direction as a citizen of a particular field, and being in a position of actually inventing a space. I got quite fortunate in that it became possible for me, through getting a job at Goldsmiths, to invent a certain kind of arena.

Then I realized that a second level was becoming apparent. What became really important to have is a space in which people could deal with what they thought to be urgent issues—without having to filter these through the prisms of disciplines and methodologies. So a group of people came together—with backgrounds in art history, in art practice, in philosophy, in critical theory, and so on—and instead of asking what materials we should look at and what methods we should use, we grouped all of our work in our teaching program around thematics and issues. We created a structure that was fluid and loose enough to change as the issues and the urgencies around it changed.

The main issue is how to think "the unbounded" intellectually. We all draw on structuralism, poststructuralism, feminism, postcolonialism, psychoanalysis, issues of performativity, as well as Deleuze—not as an author, but considered as a paradigm shift. I have some colleagues who absolutely do not adhere to Deleuze's thought, but we all recognize that he exemplifies a kind of a break in poststructuralism that is very much our moment. Let me add that the visual, for us, is not necessarily art, or visual materials. In my own recent work on "participation," instead of dealing with art I have started to think about "the manifest"—which in fact can be almost anything as it emerges as a set of material presences or effects. I realized that I needed a new language and that if I had gone on talking about arts, audiences and curators, I would be reproducing the old arguments.

The most important thing about visual culture is that it does not exist in the traditional sense of a field or a discipline. And it is extremely important to make sure that it does not start existing in a formal way. In Britain, for instance, it has become an institutional tool for bringing people together in a larger rubric, but that is not producing a field, but rather a bureaucratically convenient solution. Visual culture is operating largely as an umbrella, which is not a bad thing because there are not enough of those. It allows a lot of freedom under that umbrella, something that is rare in university life today. I am constantly asked, what is visual culture, and I say, "I don't know and that does not seem to be the right question." The question might instead be "what does it make possible?"

*The turn toward visual culture—and I assume it is still a leading paradigm of your work—not only opened up a new arena of knowledge, a new interdisciplinary research object, but it also necessitated the invention of a new methodological approach. Also, as you write in* Terra Infirma, *it necessitated the invention of a "new cultural writing."*[1] *Can you briefly elaborate on the main characteristics of these two issues—methodology and mode of writing, and the way they are connected to each other?*

Whatever disciplines we all came out of, it is fair to say that what really changed us was the encounter with a highly politicized critical theory and culture. That was the driving impulse, rather than the materials. What has been of crucial importance to us was to put that theoretical-political drive into play. In that respect, the materials that we deal with become merely a way of staging bigger issues. Methodologically, it became clear early on that we might effect a shift if we replaced the history of our objects of study with the history of those who did the studying. That was an early attempt to weld together material histories and subjectivities.

What emerged in the late 1990s and what became very influential was a strong body of theory around the performative.

We realized that this theory would allow us to bring two different things together, in the sense that the performative is never just a performative object, and it is also never just a performative subject. Rather, the crucial point is the interrelation between the two of them. As we began to understand that culture was something that took place in the here and now, the question became what fed into that very moment—who you were, what the place was, what the dominant discourses were, and what exactly these cultural objects might be. So the methodology became much less strict. Initially, everybody was kind of reconstituted out of poststructuralism, which had emerged with some quite severe operating modes. In this sense, a lot of poststructuralism maintained a model of fighting with what you came out of. The encounter with Deleuze and the encounter with performance theory moved us into a much more contemporary moment.

What is interesting about the context I work in is that we spend quite a lot of time thinking what our subject might be. Increasingly, I think that our subject is contemporaneity, and by that I do not mean contemporary materials …

*… but the question of what it means to live in the present …*

… yes. And the present, just by virtue of being the present, allows conjunctions and meeting points that would never have been permitted any time before, and might not be permitted any time after. For instance, when I work in a museum, I do not work as a curator but as a theorist—which is very important to me. I bring in philosophers, architects, activists, curators, dancers, artists, and they all work as exactly what they are. To me, that is contemporaneity—that an institution like a museum can accommodate all these different fields and allow them to develop a perfect legitimacy.

*Concerning the new mode of writing that is supposed to emerge from the expanded field of study—or contemporaneity—I was wondering about its more specific parameters. At one point, you note that your main concern is not writing* about *art but writing with art.*

I think this remains consistently important because its implications are that you are not objectifying something, or turning it into an object of your discourse. Rather, the encounter with some kind of practice throws you into a condition that furthers your thought. So you are not writing about *it*, but *it* is pushing you and pushing *at* you. You are working out something *with* it. That also does away with the centrality of the artist in establishing the meaning of a particular work. One of the reasons I remain fairly interested in artistic practice is because it is quite different from intellectual practice in that it has freedoms that intellectual practice sometimes does not. To start in the middle, to invent your own methodology and to subvert existing forms—I really like all that and I think intellectuals should work much more like artists in that sense. "Writing with art" is allowing art to upset your working processes, to point you to something you might not have been able to get to in a purely logical or systematic procedure.

An important aspect of this is writing your own subjectivity. I remember the first instance where I understood that, which was reading a book by Patricia Williams, an African-American legal theorist, *The Alchemy of Race and Rights*.[2] In the opening passage, she describes herself sitting on her bed, wearing a horrible old frayed pink bathrobe, worrying endlessly about something of considerable substance, and this conjunction brings her to the statement "that life is complicated, is a profound theoretical statement." That, for me, was a perfect instance of something prima facie simple with very important political implications. In fact, there are huge numbers of women, minorities, or non-Westerners who have no obvious point of access into discourse, so one has to invent oneself such an access. Writing your own subjectivity is not about confessing, being personal, or telling people about your biographies and life conditions. It is about finding a place to insert yourself, and you have to produce that point of access because it is not there for you.

With performance theory, we started to come across so-called performative writing. A lot of that had to do with performance artists who were taking certain liberties and producing monologues that were great theoretical treatises. For instance, the work of Peggy Phelan was incredibly important there.[3] It became very significant to try to find a voice and a mode for a particular problematic, and it continues to be a huge struggle because there is no formula for it. Recently, various people told me that when they read my texts they have the impression that I am constantly talking to myself. I think that is true, there is a kind of play of inner voices at work in writing. It also means that I am more and more inclined to write for a different audience—a public which is not necessarily exclusively an academic or an arts audience. You are writing some conversation that is going on in your head and that allows several kinds of audiences to merge.

In the 1980s and 1990s there was a vast amount of extraordinary theoretical work to take in, just in order to understand and learn. Every five minutes, you encountered another thinker, another body of thought, or another critical paradigm which radically challenged everything you had known up to then. Inevitably, what happened was that we wrote *about* theory because we were so transformed by what we were taking in. Now, we have entered a quite different moment and theory has very much become a creative practice itself. I am not writing about other theorists anymore, and even if I am excited by some of them, like Agamben or Nancy in recent years, they become just another voice in my overall collection of voices. In that respect, I am very much in tandem with Deleuze and his complete negation of state philosophy. Ninety percent of what circulates as theory is about somebody else's theory whereas I am really interested in theory as a creative practice, a practice in which something gets "created" in the process of the work.

## Situated Criticality

*Concerning the scope and internal make-up of visual culture, I was wondering if the main transformative step—the vast expansion of what used to be considered legitimate visual objects of study—was leading to a kind of countermove, viz. the emphasis on situatedness and positionality of knowledge. Do you see any connection between these two aspects of visual studies?*

I am not sure I understand your question. My sense is that the materials are really secondary to the problematic. Usually, when I start working on a question I draw from a whole variety of materials that are quite diverse and I do not worry too much where they actually come from. It is their interaction with the problematic that is important.

*But this is like opening up a very arbitrary space …*

I have never seen any problem with arbitrariness, and the truth is that I have completely stopped paying attention to that kind of critique. Anybody who took Foucault seriously at a time when it was necessary to take him seriously could not possibly ask such questions. To me, the most important aspect of visual culture is what it makes possible. Does it make possible something that was not possible before? To me, it does, at least in the way we practice it. Worries like the ones raised by *October*[4] about relativism etc. do not really concern me. In fact, I think one should be a little bit more self-conscious about one's own territorial imperatives and the fear of one's own authority being eroded. It is not possible in the 21st century to function in such an unconscious way.

*But isn't the notion of situatedness actually the anchor that keeps that kind of problem at bay and prevents the field from becoming too loose …*

No, for me, the field could never be too loose. But in fact, situatedness and positionality mean that somewhere something is anchored, and it is anchored in *you* because you are always looking at a problematic from a learned perspective and a certain set of interests. What has increasingly guided my thinking in the last couple of years is the extensive philosophical discussion around singularity—what Peter Hallward has called the move from the specific to the singular.[5] This is the move away from the logic of something being its context, the question where it comes from and where it is anchored in, toward a logic of its own internal organization. What has made singularity central in my thinking, even about geography and globalization, is not so much the internal organization of the singular. Rather, it is the fact that if you take an issue out of its site-specific contexts you allow new sorts of relations between singularities to emerge—singularities that are non-identitarian, non-located in a necessarily material sense but nevertheless located through their relations with one another, etc. In today's world, which we are beginning to understand in terms of multitude politics, in terms of circulations and mobilities, not to be anchored in a context but to have a new set of relations amongst us is particularly relevant. Jean-Luc Nancy says it is the shift from "*having* in common," like nationality, gender or ethnicity, to "*being* in common."[6] That for me is the shift of singularity. Actually, I am still struggling with this notion because I still want to think about place, but I do not want to think about it in terms of location. I am not sure if it is possible to think about place in terms of singularity but I am experimenting with it. We have developed a really urgent politics around place, but the dichotomy of the local and the global, the positioned and the universally circulating, will probably not do the whole work.

*Another transformative step that figures centrally in visual culture is the one from a "reflective mode"—reflecting about images, reading off their hidden contexts or subtexts—to what you call a "constitutive mode."[7] My question is, what exactly is being constituted by this move, beyond the mere assumption that interpretation or critical knowledge is always in a way constitutive of its object?*

With hindsight, I understand now that the move we made from reflective to constitutive was to get out of structures of representation. One of the biggest shifts of the past couple of years has been the realization that structures of representation are extraordinarily narrow and limited and, therefore, that we have to move beyond representation—something that is exceedingly difficult to do, since we do not have models for it, only hints here and there. Originally, it was, as you said, about moving away from an analytical mode of digging and unveiling and finding the truth, toward an understanding in a much more Deleuzian mode, viz. that culture is a series of effects which take place in the present; that the way those effects came about does not tell you anything about their implications; that these implications stem from the moment of their emergence in the present and the effects they in turn produce. That, in a way, was the shift from the reflective to the constitutive.

Right now, I am thinking much more about something I call "criticality"—which is not a good term because it is already inhabited by some fairly insignificant and meaningless aspects of what it might be to be "critical." What interests me about criticality is that it is a condition in which you understand that, for all the amazing amount of theoretical analysis that you have internalized and are perfectly capable of doing, you are nevertheless also living out the conditions of the situation that you critically analyze. Therefore, one has to bring these two aspects together: the ability to see through cultural modes and operations, and the lived condition that one also inhabits. It was one of the problems of poststructuralism that very often, it produced a kind of knowing outsideness—you could see through culture because you analyzed it. I am interested in the notion of "criticality" because I think we have to have both the experiential and the analytical voice. When I said that writing is a kind of dialogue in my head I meant a whole different set of positions that I occupy all the time. There are certain conditions that one literally suffers from, at the same time as being able to see through them. This, by the way, is a particularly important mode for displaced or non-Western intellectuals operating in or with the West. You are always in and out of the problematic, in and out of the audience, in and out of comprehension.

## Non-Representative Participation

*An ongoing concern in your research has been the aspect of participation—how visual culture involves or engages its audiences, how it makes them take part in its inter-textual network. Are we witnessing something like a new historical (or methodological) stage, such as from linguistic turn to textual turn to visual turn, and now to a participatory turn?*

I actually think we are in some kind of participatory turn. I see it around me and I see everybody gravitating toward it, but I do not have a full grasp of what it means across the arts and the humanities. To me, participation has a series of very specific aims. At its heart lies the question of what it means to take part in culture beyond the roles that culture allots us. We are viewers, listeners, visitors and voters, and I am interested in understanding participation not through the mode that is generated for us by certain practices, but through the kind that we invent ourselves, very often at the level of the unconscious. In that respect, I think we sometimes produce very odd participations.

There is also a quite important political dimension to this: all around us, we see the demise of the model of Western parliamentary representative democracy. In part, this demise has to do with the fact that in the last 25 years of a highly critical culture, we have atomized ourselves into numerous identities, affiliations, and identifications. In the political process, however, it is demanded of us to re-cohere ourselves into one identity, to cast one vote for one party or one person. I think that in the spaces of contemporary culture, really interesting modes of participation are developing. Instead of us emulating the model of parliamentary representative democracy, I very much think that the latter has something to learn from us.

In the last year, I have started working closely with a network of activists across Europe. One of the things I have understood from this collaboration is that there are numerous people who are participating through being fiercely communicative. There is a vast culture of communication that is a mode of participation in and of itself, that has nothing to so with communicating about this and that issue. Today, I am much less interested in the activation of the viewer, but more in the fact that there are unacknowledged and slightly mysterious modes of participating that we have not begun to fully comprehend. In that respect, I am really doing a kind of ethno-detective work which is extremely unscientific: I go to a lot of exhibitions and listen to other people's conversations, I watch how they behave and how they dress, and I try to understand how they are taking part.

One of the interesting things about participation is that wherever we gather together, whether we have something in common or not, we become a community in that very performative moment of gathering together—something which has huge implications. Art exhibitions are powerful spaces, not because they might show powerful art, or because they belong to powerful institutions, but because they are some of the few places we have that demand attention and concentration. And I would really like that attention and concentration used for something more important.

*How far can the situation that you just described really constitute a new form of collectivity?*[8] *You seem to be very much in favor of forms of community that are very fleeting and transient and are produced in the very moment of getting together. You set this strategically against notions of community that are based on a pre-existent identity. How can a very accidental coming-together, as it happens in cultural events or at art exhibitions where people do not necessarily have to share a lot beyond that very cultural interest, legitimately be called a collective?*

When I speak of collective I think of something that cannot be instrumentalized, something that cannot actually be made to operate as a collective. The point is to *read* it as a collective, to view it as a basis of operation which enables you to locate power elsewhere. That is what I am looking for. The question is, where is it that we are empowered? Thousands of people sitting there and communicating at four o'clock in the morning exemplifies a mode of empowerment. Also, people getting agitated in an exhibition can be a mode of empowerment. Of course, you cannot directly translate that into a certain kind of politics. It is more about locating spaces …

*… but is it empowerment only for the moment—say, as long as people are involved in a certain activity—or does it ever go beyond that?*

It is hard to say. What is important is not so much the continuing action, but rather the conclusions. I once had a very funny experience in London. There was a big Jackson Pollock exhibition, which I really did not want to go and see since I am bored with heroic masculinity and the notion of freedom of expression through throwing paint around. But I somehow felt obligated to visit and I asked a colleague of mine who does a lot of work on American art of the 1960s to come with me. About two minutes into the exhibition, we recognized an American television actress in the public. By sheer chance, we both happened to be big fans of the series in which this actress is in, which is *E. R.* We always watch it and talk about it the next morning at work. So we completely turned our back on Jackson Pollock and began to follow the actress around in the exhibition, talking about her, the guy she was with, the color of her hair and so on. At the end we realized we had basically substituted one structure of fandom for another. I am really interested in that kind of disassociation—being able to say that there is a larger pool of spaces that we are positioned in as fans—because I think it has potential even if I do not know how to instrumentalize it.

*With respect to the issue of participation, the aspect of "looking away"*[9] *as you also call it appears slightly paradoxical. You keep stressing particular ruptures, the distancing and distraction that might occur while viewing an exhibition, as a certain reinforcement of the participatory mode. How are we to conceive this aspect of looking away, which at first sight seems to be the complete opposite of what you try to subsume it under?*

I think it is a legacy of a certain kind of poststructuralist thought to try and undo binary relations. In the wake of that, one my concerns is to not engage in a conflictual manner. It would be easy to blast a load of critical discourse at contemporary art institutions like the Tate Modern and explain why their exhibitions are lousy and irresponsible. But I am much more interested in moving sideways and seeing things as opportunities for something else. My "looking away" is extremely strategic. It is about *not* engaging in frontal and confrontational binary structures.

When I first read about Agamben's idea of "the whatever" (as in the "whatever singularity"),[10] I thought it was very important to disassociate that from San Fernando Valley teenage-speak. But increasingly, I am thinking it is *not*. It is actually the very same thing in the hands of a serious philosopher and a bunch of teenagers. In both cases, the "whatever" means the absolute denial of the authority of the speaker, which is trying to direct a particular logic. It is about *not* allowing a dominant discourse to capture me to the extent that I will have to spend my entire time negating it. By looking away from it, I can engage with it, but in a different way. I am really fond of this notion and I think it is truly subversive.

*Couldn't "looking away" also be understood as a kind of hiding-your-head-in-the-sand strategy? For instance, in the public arena, looking away might be considered as a lack of civil courage.*

It's different, as my notion of "looking away" is very active; it is to my mind a mode of actualisation. I am just re-reading Peter Weiss' *Aesthetics of Resistance*,[11] recently translated into English, and I think it contains a very interesting description of looking away. For instance, the Pergamon altar becomes an opportunity to find another way into what the people are really preoccupied with. I think it is a highly active state and has nothing to do with withdrawal. It is about being there and being critical, but in a non-confrontational way.

## The Politics of the Bus Station

*Coming back to art exhibitions, which you have addressed as an outstanding cultural format, even as a kind of privileged stage for the new participatory mode, I wanted to ask why you see this huge potential especially in art shows, and not for instance in rock concerts or theater performances?*

I think you are right—they all are. Art exhibitions are just my natural habitat and so I am trying to maximize their potential. I think the rock concert would be an equally good example, maybe in a slightly more open way, but so is the bus station. I am interested in places where people gather together with some kind of mutuality of the moment.

*But what exactly is the political dimension of this mutuality?*

For me, the kinds of contemporary art that interest me bring up—at least sometimes when we are lucky—really important issues. Rather than seeing exhibitions as totally anchored in the art that is put on display, I think they produce conduits of access to really important issues that audiences, through their participatory strategies, complete. In that sense, they are clearly very privileged spaces. But that also highlights the importance of the curatorial, because the curatorial means that one is in charge of a field of possibilities. In a research program at Goldsmiths called "Curatorial/Knowledge," we try to think about the curatorial as an epistemic structure. In my mind, curating is not about sticking art on the wall or in spaces, but rather about making manifest structures of knowledge and accesses to issues that might not be accessible otherwise.

What I like about that way of thinking—and maybe that also characterizes visual culture—is that it starts to affect a lot of practitioners in the field. You also have to think audience and curators and artists and the space and the administrators and so on. For me, that opens up a prism through which a whole set of positions needs to be rethought. You can never really encompass it because every few months you realize that there is a new perspective that has to be taken into account. I myself started out thinking about audience and ended up thinking about curating.

*To follow up on participation once more: one aspect that really seems to stand out with respect to art exhibitions is the possibility of self-representation of a particular community or collectivity—something you have elaborated in relation to the exhibition* Black Male.[12] *Is this aspect of self-representation really the utmost or highest possible aspect that participation might amount to?*

I think not. I think it was a starting point; but what we actually begin to see now are the limits of the institutions of parliamentary representative democracy. What I now understand from the ethnography I was undertaking, which focused on the drive to make oneself the subject, is an intuitive recognition of the limits of institutional representation.

*When you wrote about* Black Male *and the scenery on the day you visited, it seemed you were very positive about the possible act of self-representation.*

What actually continues to interest me about these kinds of situations—and I have seen a lot more since—is the gesture of refusing to be represented and wanting to become the subject of the discourse oneself. If you take that further, there are huge implications for institutions of political representation and their complete impossibility. Nowadays, I would not get very excited about communities being able to represent themselves, as I did at the time of writing that text. But inasmuch as every gesture they make shows us the limits of the political institutions through which we function, I am still very interested in them.

*Coming back to the political dimension of the new participatory mode, I have a final question. Obviously, the politics of a piece of visual culture or an artwork hardly ever lies in its content or the subject matter it is dealing with. Politics also does not necessarily mean that you have to leave the realm of art and culture behind, move out into the public realm and stage some spectacle in the street. So how might participation in culture constitute a political act? Or, to pick up one of your phrases, how might a "politics without a plan" ever be made to work?*

I am very much in favor of a gestural politics, not a politics that follows an ideological map, in the sense of: this is what you believe in, and this is how you will make it come into being. Rather, I see its potentials in two directions: first, in the recuperation of textures that are kind of wasted, like being lost in a trance in front of a Rembrandt painting. As visitors in art spaces, we function in all kinds of ways whose textures are enormously important to recuperate for other kinds of activity. The other aspect is that everywhere in the West, we are operating under the edict of needing to be more and more accessible, where accessibility basically means simplicity and entertainment. In that respect, I really want to shift from the notion of accessibility to the notion of access.

So I am thinking in two directions: one is the demand that comes down on us from funding bodies, bureaucracies and governing institutions to privilege accessibility, and I think we should counter that by saying, what we need is access. The other direction of thought is all the weird textures of attention, concentration and expectation that something transformative will happen to you by looking at art, and I want to galvanize all that for different purposes.

What is really important to me is that a museum can be so much more than what it is. It is not a receptacle of artworks. It is a space of attention, a space of analysis, a space of research, a space where you can start looking at problems from a completely different perspective.

[1] Irit Rogoff, *Terra Infirma: Geography's Visual Culture*. London/New York: Routledge 2000, p. 30.

[2] Patricia J. Williams, *The Alchemy of Race and Rights*. Cambridge, Mass.: Harvard University Press 1991.

[3] Cf. Peggy Phelan, *Unmarked: The Politics of Performance*. London/New York: Routledge 1993, and Peggy Phelan & Jill Lane (eds.), *The Ends of Performance*. New York: New York University Press 1998.

[4] Cf. *October* 77 (Summer 1996), dedicated to the issue of "Visual Culture."

[5] Cf. Peter Hallward, *Absolutely Postcolonial: Writing Between the Singular and the Specific*. Manchester: Manchester University Press 2002.

[6] Cf. Jean-Luc Nancy, *Being Singular Plural*. Stanford: Stanford University Press 2000.

[7] Irit Rogoff, *Terra Infirma*, p. 9.

[8] Cf. Irit Rogoff, "We – Collectivities, Mutualities, Participations (2002)," http://theater.kein.org/node/95.

[9] Cf. Irit Rogoff, "Looking Away – Participations in Visual Culture," in *Texte zur Kunst* Heft 36, (December 1999), as well as *Looking Away – Participations in Visual Culture*. Forthcoming, MIT Press.

[10] Cf. Giorgio Agamben, *The Coming Community*. Minneapolis, London: University of Minnesota Press 1993.

[11] Peter Weiss, *The Aesthetics of Resistance. Volume 1*. Durham, London: Duke University Press 2005.

[12] *Black Male*, Whitney Museum of American Art, 1994.

# Biographies

TARIQ ALI was born in Lahore, now in Pakistan, then part of British-ruled India, in 1944. While at Punjab University, Ali organized public demonstrations against Pakistan's military dictatorship, and was consequently banned from participating in student politics. At the urging of his uncle, a member of the Pakistani Military Intelligence, Ali was sent abroad to continue his studies, as his radicalism put him at risk of imprisonment. In Britain he studied Politics, Philosophy and Economics at Exeter College, Oxford. At the height of the Vietnam War, Ali earned a national reputation through debates with figures like Henry Kissinger. Ali has written over a dozen books on world history and politics, and five novels. His most recent books include: *The Book of Saladin* (Verso, 1998); *Masters of the Universe: NATO's Balkan Crusade* (Verso, 2000); *The Clash of Fundamentalisms: Crusades, Jihad, and Modernity* (Verso, 2002); *Bush in Babylon* (Verso, 2003); *A Sultan in Palermo* (Verso, 2005); *Street-Fighting Years: An Autobiography of the Sixties* (Verso 2005); *Pirates of the Caribbean: Axis of Hope* (Verso, 2006); and *The Duel: Pakistan on the Flight Path of American Power* (Simon and Schuster, 2008). Ali is a regular contributor to and editor of the *New Left Review*; he also writes for *Monthly Review*, *Z Magazine* and *Counterpunch*. Placing himself in the front lines of the anti-war movement, he has spoken out loudly against the US military incursions into Iraq and Afghanistan.

BILL AYERS is Distinguished Professor of Education and Senior University Scholar at the University of Illinois at Chicago (UIC), and founder of both the Small Schools Workshop and the Center for Youth and Society. He teaches courses in interpretive and qualitative research and urban school change, as well as teaching and the modern predicament. Ayers has written extensively about social justice, democracy and education, the political and cultural contexts of schooling, and the meaning-making and ethical purposes of students and families and teachers. Edited books include: with Pat Ford, *City Kids/City Teachers: Reports from the Front Row* (The New Press, 1996); with Jean Ann Hunt and Therese Quinn, *Teaching for Social Justice: A Democracy and Education Reader* (The New Press and Teachers College Press, 1998); with Rick Ayers and Bernardine Dohrn, *Zero Tolerance: Resisting the*

*Drive for Punishment—A handbook for parents, students, educators and citizens* (The New Press, 2001); with Bernardine Dohrn and Jeff Jones, *Sing a Battle Song: The Revolutionary Poetry, Statements, and Communiqués of the Weather Underground 1970–1974* (Seven Stories Press, 2006); with Gloria Ladson-Billings, Pedro Noguera, and Gregory Michie, *City Kids/ City Schools: More Reports From the Front Row* ( The New Press, 2008); and with Therese Quinn and David Stovall, *The Handbook of Social Justice in Education* (Routledge, 2008). Recent books include: *Fugitive Days: A Memoir* (Beacon Press, 2001); *On the Side of the Child: Summerhill Revisited* (Teachers College Press, 2003); *Teaching the Personal and the Political: Essays on Hope and Justice* (Teachers College Press, 2004); *Teaching Toward Freedom: Moral Commitment and Ethical Action in the Classroom* (Beacon Press, 2004); and with Bernardine Dohrn, *Race Course: Against White Supremacy* (Third World Press, 2008).

ZYGMUNT BAUMAN, born in 1925 in Poland, is Emeritus Professor of Sociology at the University of Leeds, having served as Professor of Sociology and, at various times, Head of Department until his retirement in 1990. He was formerly at the University of Warsaw until 1968, and the University of Tel Aviv. He was awarded the Amalfi European Prize in 1990 and the Adorno Prize in 1998. Zygmunt Bauman is known throughout the world for works such as *Legislators and Interpreters* (Cornell University Press, 1987), *Modernity and the Holocaust* (Polity Press, 1989), *Modernity and Ambivalence* (Polity Press, 1991), and *Postmodern Ethics* (Blackwell, 1993). He is the author of more than 20 books in English and of numerous articles and reviews. His reputation, although already well-established by the 1970s in Western Europe and North America as well as throughout the then Eastern Bloc, grew at an especially rapid rate in the late 1980s. Bauman has been influential in demystifying and providing a sociological understanding of postmodernity, and he has explicitly turned to politics in his most recently published books and essays. These include: *Work, Consumerism and the New Poor* (Open University Press, 1998); *Globalisation: The Human Consequences* (Polity Press, 1998); *In Search of Politics* (Polity Press, 1999); *Liquid Modernity* (Polity Press, 2000); *Society Under Siege* (Polity Press, 2002); *Liquid Love: On the*

*Frailty of Human Bonds* (Polity Press, 2003); *Wasted Lives: Modernity and Its Outcasts* (2003); *Liquid Life* (Polity Press, 2005); *Liquid Fear* (Polity Press, 2006); *Consuming Life* (Polity Press, 2007); *Liquid Times: Living in an Age of Uncertainty* (Polity Press, 2007); *The Art of Life* (Polity Press, 2008); *and Living on Borrowed Time: Conversations with Citlali Rovirosa-Madrazo* (Polity Press, 2009).

PAUL GILROY is a noted sociologist and cultural theorist whose groundbreaking work has explored such topics as the concept of race, black nationalism, and the literature, music and cultures of the African diaspora. He taught at Goldsmiths College, London, before joining the Yale faculty in the Department of African American Studies in 1999, and The London School of Economics and Political Science in 2005. Gilroy has focused his current research on such topics as black European identity and the relationships between multiculturalism and hierarchy, the development of black vernacular and popular cultures, and the workings of colonial governance. He is internationally known for his Cultural-Studies approach in questioning purist notions of Western civilization and rigid definitions of nationalism. Gilroy's books include: *There Ain't No Black in the Union Jack: The Cultural Politics of Race and Nation* (Hutchinson, 1987); *The Black Atlantic: Modernity and Double Consciousness* (Harvard University Press, 1993); *Between Camps: Nations, Cultures and the Allure of Race* (The Penguin Press, 2000); *After Empire: Melancholia or Convivial Culture?* (Routledge, 2004); *Black Britain: A Photographic History* (co-edited with Stuart Hall, Saqi Books, 2007); and *Darker Than Blue: On The Moral Economies of Black Atlantic Cultures* (Harvard University Press, 2010).

Also a freelance journalist and a musician, Gilroy has written extensively about the expressive cultures of the African diaspora, and his articles have appeared in such publications as *The Encyclopedia of Rock*, *Sight and Sound*, *New Musical Express*, *The Wire* and *City Limits*, among others.

JEAN-PIERRE GORIN received his baccalaureate in Philosophy in 1960. He prepared for L'Ecole Normale Supérieure (rue d'Ulm) at the Lycée Louis-le-Grand from

1960 to 1964 while pursuing his Licence de Philosophie at the University of Paris (Sorbonne). He took part in the seminars of Louis Althusser, Jacques Lacan and Michel Foucault and collaborated on the creation of *Les Cahiers Marxistes-Léninistes* and *Les Cahiers pour L'analyse*. In 1965, Gorin joined the editorial staff of *Le Monde*, working for its literary department and collaborating on the creation of its weekly literary supplement (*Le Monde des livres*). He wrote more than forty articles, reviewing some of the essential writers and thinkers of the period. In 1966, he met the filmmaker Jean-Luc Godard. Two years later, they created the Dziga Vertov Group. From 1968 to 1972, Gorin co-directed the films *Wind from the East* (1969), *Struggle in Italy* (1970), *Vladimir and Rosa* (1971), *Tout Va Bien* (1972), and *Letter to Jane* (1972). The films of the Dziga Vertov Group have long been recognized as seminal to the period of radical filmmaking of the late 1960s and early 1970s. They are historically significant for their pioneering of a critical re-examination of film language and its ideological implications. Gorin joined the faculty of the Visual Arts Department of the University of California in San Diego in 1975. His investigation of narrative led him toward documentary. He attempted to redefine the parameters of the genre in a series of three essay films done in and around San Diego, which form a Southern California trilogy: *Poto and Cabengo* (1978); *Routine Pleasures* (1986); and *My Crasy Life* (1991).

LAWRENCE GROSSBERG is currently the Morris Davis Distinguished Professor of Communication Studies and Cultural Studies, and the Director of the University Program in Cultural Studies at the University of North Carolina at Chapel Hill. He is an internationally renowned scholar of Cultural Studies, having helped to introduce it to the international field of communication and the broader international academic community. He is also widely known for his work in the study of popular culture, especially popular music and youth culture, the philosophy of culture and communication, and postmodernism. His current work focuses on neoconservatism, economics and globalization on the one hand, and the modernist foundations of communication and cultural theory on the other.

He is the co-editor of the international journal *Cultural Studies*. He has authored or edited (alone or with others) 20 books, and published close to 200 essays. His books include: *It's a Sin: Essays on Postmodernism, Politics and Culture* (Power Publications, 1988); *We Gotta Get Out Of This Place: Popular Conservatism and Postmodern Culture* (Routledge, 1992); *Dancing in Spite of Myself: Essays in Popular Culture* (Duke University Press, 1997); *Bringing It All Back Home: Essays in Cultural Studies* (Duke University Press, 1997); and *Caught in the Crossfire: Kids, Politics and America's Future* (Paradigm, 2005). His co-edited books include: *Marxism and the Interpretation of Culture* (University of Illinois Press, 1987); *Cultural Studies* (Routledge, 1991); *Sound and Vision* (Routledge, 1993), *Without Guarantees: In Honor of Stuart Hall* (Verso, 2000); and *New Keywords: A Revised Vocabulary of Culture and Society* (Blackwell, 2005).

STUART HALL has been a leading figure of the British Left over the past thirty years. He is a visionary theorist whose work has made possible multiple conversations taking place around questions of culture, race and ethnicity. He was born in Kingston, Jamaica in 1932 and moved to England in 1951. A socialist, he joined forces with E. P. Thompson, Raphael Samuel, Ralph Miliband, Raymond Williams and John Saville in the 1950s to launch two radical journals, *The New Reasoner* and *New Left Review*. In 1957, Hall joined the Campaign for Nuclear Disarmament (CND). In 1964, he co-authored *The Popular Arts*. This resulted in his being invited by Richard Hoggart to join the Centre for Contemporary Cultural Studies at Birmingham University. In 1968, Hall became director of the Contemporary Cultural Studies unit. Over the next few years, he wrote and edited several books including *Situating Marx: Evaluations and Departures* (co-edited, Chaucer Pub., 1972), *Encoding and Decoding in the Television Discourse* (Centre for Contemporary Cultural Studies, 1973), *Reading of Marx's 1857 Introduction to the* Grundrisse (Centre for Contemporary Cultural Studies,1973), *Resistance Through Rituals* (co-edited, Hutchinson, 1976), and *Policing the Crisis* (co-edited, Palgrave Macmillan, 1978). In 1979, Hall was appointed as professor of sociology at the Open University. Other important books by Hall include: *The Hard Road to Renewal* (Verso, 1988), *New Times* (co-edited,

Lawrence & Wishart, 1989); *The Formation of Modernity* (co-edited, Blackwell, 1992), *Modernity and Its Future* (co-edited, Blackwell, 1992); *Stuart Hall: Critical Dialogues in Cultural Studies* (Routledge, 1996); *Questions of Cultural Identity* (co-edited, Sage Publications, 1996); *Representation: Cultural Representations and Signifying Practices* (Sage Publications, 1997); *Visual Culture: The Reader* (co-edited, Sage Publications, 1999); and *Different* (Phaidon Press, 2001).

DAVID HARVEY is a leading theorist in the field of urban studies. He earned his Ph.D. from Cambridge University, was formerly professor of geography at Johns Hopkins, a Miliband Fellow at the London School of Economics, and the Halford Mackinder Professor of Geography at Oxford, and is now a Distinguished Professor of Anthropology at the City University of New York. Harvey's research interests encompass geography, Marxism and social theory, urban planning and architecture, social justice, and utopianism. His highly influential books include: *Social Justice and the City* (Johns Hopkins University Press, 1973); *Limits to Capital* (Blackwell, 1982); *The Urbanization of Capital* (Johns Hopkins University Press, 1985); *The Condition of Postmodernity* (Blackwell, 1990); *Justice, Nature, and the Geography of Difference* (Blackwell, 1996); *Spaces of Hope* (University of California Press, 2000); *Spaces of Capital: Towards a Critical Geography* (Edinburgh University Press, 2001); *The New Imperialism* (Oxford University Press, 2003); *Paris, Capital of Modernity* (Routledge, 2003); *A Brief History of Neoliberalism* (Oxford University Press, 2005); *Spaces of Global Capitalism: A Theory of Uneven Geographical Development* (Verso, 2006); *Cosmopolitanism and the Geographies of Freedom* (Columbia University Press, 2009); and *A Companion to Marx's* Capital (Verso, 2009). His numerous awards include the Outstanding Contributor Award of the Association of American Geographers and the 2002 Centenary Medal of the Royal Scottish Geographical Society for his "outstanding contribution to the field of geographical enquiry and to anthropology." He holds honorary degrees from the universities of Buenos Aires, Roskilde in Denmark, Uppsala in Sweden, and Ohio State University.

ACHILLE MBEMBE, born in Cameroon, obtained his Ph.D. in History at the Sorbonne in Paris in 1989 and a D.E.A. in Political Science at the Institut d'Etudes Politiques (Paris). He was Assistant Professor of History at Columbia University, New York, from 1988 to 1991; a Senior Research Fellow at the Brookings Institute in Washington, D.C., from 1991 to 1992; Associate Professor of History at the University of Pennsylvania from 1992 to 1996; and Executive Director of the Council for the Development of Social Science Research in Africa (CODESRIA) in Dakar, Senegal, from 1996 to 2000. Mbembe was also a Visiting Professor at the University of California, Berkeley, in 2001, and a Visiting Professor at Yale University in 2003. He is currently Senior Researcher at the Wits Institute for Social and Economic Research at the University of Witwatersrand, Johannesburg, South Africa. He has written extensively on African history and politics, including the books *Afriques indociles* (Karthala 1988), and *La naissance du maquis dans le Sud-Cameroun* (Karthala, 1996). His book, *On the Postcolony*, published in French in 2000 (Karthala), and in English in 2001 (University of California Press), was the winner of the 2006 Bill Venter/ Altron Literary Award. His latest book, *Johannesburg: The Elusive Metropolis* (co-edited with Sarah Nuttal), was brought out by Duke University Press in 2008.

MEAGHAN MORRIS is Chair Professor of Cultural Studies and Coordinator of the Kwan Fong Cultural Research and Development Programme at Lingnan University, Hong Kong. She is an internationally acclaimed scholar with a long-standing reputation for innovative and immensely influential work in Film and Media Studies, Historical Cultural Studies, Gender Studies and Australian and Asian-Pacific Popular Culture. Her books include: *Michel Foucault: Power, Truth, Strategy* (co-edited with Paul Patton, Feral Publications, 1978); *The Pirate's Fiancée: Feminism, Reading, Postmodernism* (Routledge, 1988); *Australian Cultural Studies: A Reader* (co-edited with John Frow, University of Illinois Press, 1993); *Too Soon, Too Late: History in Popular Culture* (Indiana University Press, 1998); *"Race" Panic and the Memory of Migration* (co-edited with Brett de Bary, University of Washington Press, 2001); *New Keywords: a Revised Vocabulary of Culture and Society* (co-edited with Tony Bennett and Lawrence Grossberg, Blackwell, 2005); and *Hong Kong Connections: Transnational Imagination in Action Cinema* (co-edited with Stephen Chan and Siu Leung Li, Hong Kong University Press, 2005). Her latest book, *Identity Anecdotes: Translation and Media Culture*, was brought out by Sage Publications in 2006. She is Senior Editor of *Traces: a Multilingual Journal of Cultural Theory and Translation*, and Chair of the International Association for Cultural Studies.

ELLA SHOHAT is Professor in the departments of Art and Public Policy and Middle Eastern Studies at New York University. She has lectured and published extensively on the intersection of gender, post/colonialism, and multiculturalism, as well as on Zionist discourse, and the Arab-Jewish and Mizrahi question. Her award-winning publications include: *Israeli Cinema: East/West and the Politics of Representation* (University of Texas Press, 1989); *Unthinking Eurocentrism: Multiculturalism and the Media* (with Robert Stam, Routledge, 1994); *Dangerous Liaisons: Gender, Nation and Postcolonial Perspectives* (co-edited, University of Minnesota Press, 1997); *Talking Visions: Multicultural Feminism in a Transnational Age* (MIT Press & the New Museum, 1998); *Multiculturalism, Postcoloniality and Transnational Media* (co-edited, Rutgers University Press, 2003); *Taboo Memories, Diasporic Voices* (Duke University Press, 2006); and *Flagging Patriotism: Crises of Narcissism and Anti-Americanism* (with Robert Stam, Routledge, 2006). Ella Shohat has served on the editorial board of such journals as *Social Text*, *Public Culture*, *Jouvert* and *Critique* and has curated a number of cultural programs both nationally and internationally. Her writing has been translated into several languages, including French, Spanish, Portuguese, Arabic, Hebrew, German, Polish, and Turkish.

IRIT ROGOFF is Professor of Visual Cultures at Goldsmiths College, London. She writes extensively on the conjunctions of contemporary art with critical theory, with particular reference to issues of colonialism, cultural difference and performativity. Rogoff has been director of the international AHRB research project *Translating the Image: Cross-cultural Contemporary Arts* housed at Goldsmiths College (2001 to 2006), and is a member of the editorial boards of *Parallax*

(University of Leeds) and *Visual Culture* (Sage Publications). She is the author of *Terra Infirma: Geography's Visual Culture* (Routledge, 2000), editor of *The Divided Heritage: Themes and Problems in German Modernism* (Cambridge University Press, 1991) and co-editor, with Daniel Sherman, of *Museum Culture: Histories, Theories, Spectacles* (University of Minnesota Press, 1994). Her forthcoming books include: *Looking Away: Participations in Visual Culture* (MIT Press); and *Othering German Art: Haunts of Difference* (University of California Press).

## About the editors

CHRISTIAN HÖLLER is editor of *springerin – Hefte für Gegenwartskunst* (www.springerin.at) and has written extensively on art and cultural theory. In 2000, he curated the special program *Pop Unlimited? Image Transfer and Image Production in Contemporary Pop Culture* at the 46th International Short Film Festival in Oberhausen, Germany. Between 2002 and 2007, he has been Visiting Professor at the Geneva University of Art and Design (formerly Ecole supérieure des beaux-arts). In 2006–07, he has been editor of *documenta 12 magazines*; in 2009, sub-curator of the exhibition *See This Sound* (Lentos Kunstmuseum Linz; section "Site Sound Industry"); in 2010, curator of the program *No Wave 1976–84* (56th International Short Film Festival in Oberhausen and Austrian Filmmuseum, Vienna). In 2001, he edited the anthology *Pop Unlimited?* (Turia + Kant, Vienna); in 2005, the volume *Techno-Visionen* (Folio, Vienna/Bolzano; together with Sandro Droschl und Harald A. Wiltsche) as well as the monographic catalogue *Hans Weigand* (Verlag der Buchhandlung Walther König, Cologne).

ANNE-JULIE RACCOURSIER received her diploma at the Ecole supérieure d'arts visuels in Geneva in 1999 and a Master of Fine Arts in Critical Studies from the California Institute of the Arts in 2003. While continuing her artistic practice, she has worked as Coordinator Assistant of the CCC Postgraduate Study Program at the Geneva University of Art and design (formerly Ecole supérieure des beaux-arts) from 2003 to 2006. During this time, she collaborated with Christian Höller on editing this publication.

# Imprint

Edited by Anne-Julie Raccoursier
Research-Based Master Programme CCC—Critical Curatorial Cybermedia, Geneva University of Art and Design/Haute école d'art et de design – Genève

COPY EDITING
Tim Jones

DESIGN CONCEPT
Gavillet & Rust, Geneva

DESIGN
Nicola Todeschini

TYPEFACE
Genath

PRINT AND BINDING
EBS Editoriale Bortolazzi-Stei, Verona

This book has been realized with the support of Geneva University of Art and Design/Haute école d'art et de design – Genève

—HEAD GENÈVE

Hes·so
Haute Ecole Spécialisée de Suisse occidentale
Fachhochschule Westschweiz
University of Applied Sciences Western Switzerland

PUBLISHED BY
JRP|Ringier
Letzigraben 134
CH–8047 Zurich
T +41 43 311 27 50
F +41 43 311 27 51
E info@jrp-ringier.com
www.jrp-ringier.com

IN CO-EDITION WITH
Les presses du réel
35 rue Colson
F–21000 Dijon
T +33 3 80 30 75 23
F +33 3 80 30 59 74
E info@lespressesdureel.com
www.lespressesdureel.com

ISBN 978-3-03764-124-8 (JRP|Ringier)
ISBN 978-2-84066-396-6 (Les presses du réel)

## Distribution

GERMANY AND AUSTRIA
Vice Versa Vertrieb, Immanuelkirchstrasse 12, D-10405 Berlin, info@vice-versa-vertrieb.de, www.vice-versa-vertrieb.de

FRANCE
Les presses du réel, 35 rue Colson, F-21000 Dijon, info@lespressesdureel.com, www.lespressesdureel.com

SWITZERLAND
Buch 2000, AVA Verlagsauslieferung AG, Centralweg 16, CH-8910 Affoltern a.A., buch2000@ava.ch, www.ava.ch

UK AND OTHER EUROPEAN COUNTRIES
Cornerhouse Publications, 70 Oxford Street, UK-Manchester M1 5NH, publications@cornerhouse.org, www.cornerhouse.org/books

USA, CANADA, ASIA, AND AUSTRALIA
D.A.P./Distributed Art Publishers, 155 Sixth Avenue, 2nd Floor, USA-New York, NY 10013, dap@dapinc.com, www.artbook.com

Documents Series 5:
Christian Höller

This book is the fifth volume in the “Documents” series, dedicated to critics’ writings.

The series is directed by Lionel Bovier and Xavier Douroux.

## Also available

DOCUMENTS SERIES (IN ENGLISH)

Saul Anton, *Warhol's Dream*
ISBN 978-3-905770-35-3 (JRP|Ringier)
ISBN 978-2-84066-200-6 (Les presses du réel)

Bob Nickas, *Theft Is Vision*
ISBN 978-3-905770-36-0 (JRP|Ringier)
ISBN 978-2-84066-206-8 (Les presses du réel)

Hans Ulrich Obrist, *A Brief History of Curating*
ISBN 978-3-905829-55-6 (JRP|Ringier)
ISBN 978-2-84066-287-7 (Les presses du réel)

Dorothea von Hantelmann, *How to Do Things with Art*
ISBN 978-3-03764-104-0 (JRP|Ringier)
ISBN 978-2-84066-361-4 (Les presses du réel)

DOCUMENTS SUR L'ART (IN FRENCH)

Daniel Birnbaum, *Chronologie*
ISBN 978-2-84066-165-8 (Les presses du réel)
ISBN 978-3-905770-98-8 (JRP|Ringier)

Diedrich Diederichsen, *Argument son*
ISBN 978-2-84066-140-5 (Les presses du réel)
ISBN 978-3-905829-00-6 (JRP|Ringier)

Stéphanie Moisdon, *Stéphanie Moisdon*
ISBN 978-2-84066-205-1 (Les presses du réel)
ISBN 978-3-905829-15-0 (JRP|Ringier)

Hans Ulrich Obrist, *… dontstopdontstopdontstopdontstop*
ISBN 978-2-84066-222-8 (Les presses du réel)
ISBN 978-3-905829-14-3 (JRP|Ringier)